SPIRIT WORKS

CYCLE C SERMONS FOR
PENTECOST SUNDAY
THROUGH PROPER 12
BASED ON THE GOSPEL TEXTS

ROBERT C. COCHRAN

CSS PUBLISHING COMPANY, INC.
LIMA, OHIO

SPIRIT WORKS

FIRST EDITION
Copyright © 2015
by CSS Publishing Co., Inc.

Library of Congress Cataloging-in-Publication Data

Cochran, Robert C.
  Spirit works : Cycle C sermons for Pentecost Sunday through proper 12 : based on the
gospel texts / Robert C. Cochran. -- First edition.
    pages cm
  ISBN 0-7880-2819-7 (alk. paper)
  1. Bible. Gospels--Sermons. 2. Sermons, American--21st century. 3. Pentecost season--
Sermons. 4. Church year sermons. 5. Common lectionary (1992). Year C. I. Title.

  BS2555.54.C63 2014
  252'.64--dc23

                                                          2014038678

For more information about CSS Publishing Company resources, visit our web-
site at www.csspub.com, email us at csr@csspub.com, or call (800) 241-4056.

e-book
ISBN-13: 978-0-7880-2820-5
ISBN-10: 0-7880-2820-0

ISBN-13: 978-0-7880-2819-9
ISBN-10: 0-7880-2819-7   PRINTED IN USA

I would like to dedicate these works of the Spirit to my wife, Pam; my parents, C.P. and Donna; and my congregation, First Lutheran Church of Findlay, Ohio, for their infinite patience and good humor.

This is the first title written by Robert Cochran
for CSS Publishing Company, Inc.

TABLE OF CONTENTS

Pentecost Sunday
John 14:8-17 (25-27)

Philip said to [Jesus], "Lord, show us the Father, and we will be satisfied." Jesus said to him, "Have I been with you all this time, Philip, and you still do not know me? Whoever has seen me has seen the Father. How can you say, 'Show us the Father'? Do you not believe that I am in the Father and the Father is in me? The words that I say to you I do not speak on my own; but the Father who dwells in me does his works. Believe me that I am in the Father and the Father is in me; but if you do not, then believe me because of the works themselves. Very truly, I tell you, the one who believes in me will also do the works that I do and, in fact, will do greater works than these, because I am going to the Father. I will do whatever you ask in my name, so that the Father may be glorified in the Son. If in my name you ask me for anything, I will do it. If you love me, you will keep my commandments. And I will ask the Father, and he will give you another Advocate, to be with you forever. This is the Spirit of truth, whom the world cannot receive, because it neither sees him nor knows him. You know him, because he abides with you, and he will be in you. I have said these things to you while I am still with you. But the Advocate, the Holy Spirit, whom the Father will send in my name, will teach you everything, and remind you of all that I have said to you. Peace I leave with you; my peace I give to you. I do not give to you as the world gives. Do not let your hearts be troubled, and do not let them be afraid."

WE ARE NOT ALONE

This is the day of Pentecost, when we celebrate the gift of the Holy Spirit. In honor of this, I decided to not prepare a sermon today. Instead, I'm just going to stand here and let the Holy Spirit tell me what to say. Uh....

As Christians, we are not to become empty-headed ventriloquist dummies sitting on the Holy Spirit's lap: we need to continue to use our God-given minds. Some would disagree with this, believing that the Holy Spirit works solely through the emotions. The Holy Spirit thus becomes the "Holy Spouter." From this perspective, one can tell when people are in the throes of the Holy Spirit because it just comes gushing from them. If you don't experience outbursts of religious ecstasy, you're not really in touch with the Holy Spirit.

We Lutherans and many others in the mainline tradition hear the charge all the time that our faith is too quiet, too passive. Actually, I'll admit we do often seem restrained: we seldom allow the Holy Spirit to stir us in any obvious way.

The story is told of the stranger who comes to a Lutheran church for the first time, and when the pastor is just a few minutes into his sermon, the man suddenly shouts out, "Praise the Lord!" The congregation gasps, the pastor grabs at his heart and knocks his notes to the floor. Gathering himself, the pastor goes on, but a little while later the man cries, "Amen!" The congregation gasps again and starts mumbling among themselves. The pastor is clearly shaken but manages to soldier on. Things have just settled down again when the man screams, "Preach it, brother!"

This time, one of the ushers comes running up the aisle and tells the stranger, "Look, sir, this is a Lutheran church, you have to keep quiet." "But I have the Spirit within me!" the man declares. "Well you didn't get it here!" the usher assures him.

If Garrison Keillor (*A Prairie Home Companion*) has taught us anything, it is that Lutherans can take a joke, even if it is at their own expense. And, goodness knows, we aren't perfect. But in this case, the calmness of our faith may not be a problem. The Spirit also moves quietly. The most common biblical metaphor for the Spirit is the wind. Winds range from tempests to breezes, and a summer breeze can move one's heart as much as a winter blast. Sometimes those who are enamored with stormy religiosity miss the subtle movements of the Spirit.

Have you ever read the end of the book of Matthew? Matthew ends after the resurrection with Jesus telling his disciples to "Go therefore and make disciples of all nations, baptizing them in the name of the Father and of the Son and of the Holy Spirit, and teaching them to obey everything that I have commanded you" (Matthew 28:19-20) His final words are, "And remember, I am with you always, to the end of the age" (Matthew 28:20). And then he leaves! In the words of our creeds, he ascends to sit at the right hand of the Father.

Has this ever struck you as odd? Douglas MacArthur vowed, "I shall return." Arnold Schwarzenegger threatened, "I'll be back!" But Jesus said he'd always be with us. The book of Matthew begins with an angel telling Joseph that Mary will bear a child who will be called "Emmanuel": Emmanuel means "God is with us." The assumption is that, unlike Elvis, Jesus is not leaving the building! (After every Elvis Presley concert someone would announce that Elvis had left the building, so the faithful would finally go home.)

Today's gospel lesson is part of Jesus' long good-bye to his disciples in John that begins in 13:33, "Little children, I am with you only a little longer," and doesn't end until his prayer for the disciples in chapter 17 and subsequent arrest in chapter 18. One gets the feeling that the disciples didn't want their champion to depart. But Jesus could do more than just promise he'd be back: he could promise they'd never again be alone because he would have the Father send the Holy Spirit.

Today's first reading describes the coming of the Holy Spirit upon the disciples on the day of Pentecost after Jesus' death. Before we can comprehend this, we need to understand what the Holy Spirit is. Throughout the ages, there have always been misconceptions and false teachings about the Holy Spirit. The key is that the Holy Spirit cannot be thought of without reference to the Father and the Son. Far too often, the Spirit is "worshiped and glorified" as if the third person of the Trinity possesses a life separate from the first and second. Obsession with the Spirit can get one into a lot of trouble.

We are all called to open ourselves to the workings of the Spirit, and sometimes pensive Christians are afraid to do this, but as today's gospel says, the main task of the Spirit is to remind us of everything Jesus taught about the Father. The Spirit, then, does not lead us away from careful study of the scriptures and doesn't condemn thoughtful worship or regard quiet, humble service as trite. We are not being asked to abandon our minds in favor of our emotions. The Spirit is certainly demonstrated in ecstatic prayers, faith healings, and speaking in tongues but is also evident in Bible studies, in many forms of worship, in contemplative prayers, and in the loving ways we treat each other.

So, if the Spirit is not to be thought of as a separate being from the Father and the Son, how are we to think of it? One of my professors at Trinity Lutheran Seminary in Columbus, Ohio, told of a lengthy course he once taught on the

11

Trinity in his church. After weeks of very intense and learned discussion, an elderly woman who hadn't said anything told the group that she always thought of the Trinity as a marble cake: one cake with three distinct strands that can't be pulled apart without destroying the whole. My professor threw up his hands and said, "Good enough, class is over!"

So, what does this strand that is the Holy Spirit look like? Who did Jesus send to us as we await the second coming? Jesus says that the Father will send an advocate for us in his absence. The Greek word that our version translates as "advocate" is *paraklatos*, paraclete. Literally, a paraclete is "one who stands alongside." The divine paraclete is here to defend us when no one else will, to teach us what we don't know, and to help us do what we need to do. In addition, the Spirit is here to build us up when our morale is low and give us new hope.

Perhaps the lowest point of my life so far occurred when I failed to finish my dissertation in English literature in the allotted time, and my doctoral program crumbled around me. A two-year relationship had just ended, and friends and favorite teachers just walked away. There was nothing for me to do but leave school and move back to my parent's house with nothing to show for the time I'd spent in school but a wonderful cat I'd adopted named Marlowe.

One night, with everyone gone, I opened the door to let Marlowe in, but he just stood there. His mouth had a cut on it, so I figured he'd been in a fight. I took him up in my arms and called a veterinarian, who agreed to meet me at his office though it was late. All the way there, Marlowe wrapped himself warmly around my arm and rested quietly. The vet looked him over and said that it really didn't look like he had been in a fight. Marlowe didn't move until the doctor opened his mouth, and then he let out a terrible cry.

The doctor told me to go home, he'd take some x-rays, and call me. He called me shortly after I got home and told me that Marlowe had a crushed skull. He'd been hit by a car, and the doctor asked for permission to put him to sleep. I fell asleep that night crying, "Now, they've killed my cat!"

The next morning, I heard my nephew, Cody and my niece, Aubrey Jo coming up the stairs after church. I really wanted to be left alone that morning. But five-year-old Cody tiptoed in and showed me a picture he'd drawn in Sunday school of me and Marlowe. "Thank you, Cody, that's wonderful," I said. Little Aubrey, three years old at the time, came thumping up the stairs after him, banged open the door, marched up to my bed and announced, "Your cat is dead."

My mouth dropped open and after I gathered myself, I said, "Yes, Aubrey, that's true." "A car hit him and cracked his head open!" she proclaimed and shook her head once, decisively. God had sent an advocate to help me, but she wasn't exactly the kind of angel I was expecting, nor did she come with the kind of message I was looking for.

At that moment, I thought of myself as a tragic figure, but Aubrey turned the moment from high tragedy to low comedy. I wanted someone to come and tell me all the deep, hidden meaning behind what had happened, instead Jesus sent the Spirit in the form of a little cherub to remind me that real tragedies require a noble hero who falls through no fault of his/her own. We, however, more closely resemble characters in a farce, who are funny because they consider themselves tragic figures but are neither noble nor faultless. They are bounders and fools pretending to be kings and heroes. And so are we.

The reality check that Aubrey gave me was more valuable than any sympathetic shoulder could have been at that moment: "Your cat's dead: what are you going to do about it?" I grabbed Aubrey and the three of us wrestled and bounced on the bed until it was time to eat.

The "why" is of little significance when a cat gets run over, when a girlfriend leaves and friends betray, or a dissertation isn't written. The question is, "What are you going to do about it?" What I ended up doing about it was visiting Trinity Lutheran Seminary. In a sense, I stand here today because of all the rotten things that happened to me during that period in my life. And none of those things hold any importance to me now. Through the workings of the Spirit, I have moved on.

Besides defending, teaching, motivating, and uplifting, it is the Spirit that unites us. Remember the tower of Babel? In this story people's obsessions with their own personal power cause them to try and build a tower to the heavens to glorify themselves. Their attempt only gets them defeated and divided. Their arrogance forces God to confuse their tongues, giving them different languages so they won't try it again.

Today, we heard that when the Spirit came at Pentecost, fiery tongues settled on each person in the room. When the Spirit took control of them, they didn't speak in the same language: they communicated in whatever language the Spirit gave them the power to speak. The lesson is that it is the Spirit that enables us to communicate with anyone to "Go therefore and make disciples of *all* nations," regardless of what languages they speak: to communicate with the rich and the homeless, Moslems and Buddhists, seniors and teenagers!

We are not alone: Jesus has not left the building. An advocate has been sent who will defend us, teach us, encourage us, renew us, and unite us. Pray that the Spirit comes to this place that we might go out and reach others. Next week is Holy Trinity Sunday. To an unchurched observer, it might seem that the Fundamentalists worship God the Father, we Lutherans (with our relentless emphasis on God's grace) worship the Son, and the Pentecostals worship the Holy Spirit. Today, I would urge us all to reclaim the Holy Spirit in our religious life because, after all, it is through the Spirit that the Father and Son come to us.

Holy Trinity Sunday
John 16:12-15

I still have many things to say to you, but you cannot bear them now. When the Spirit of truth comes, he will guide you into all the truth; for he will not speak on his own, but will speak whatever he hears, and he will declare to you the things that are to come. He will glorify me, because he will take what is mine and declare it to you. All that the Father has is mine. For this reason I said that he will take what is mine and declare it to you.

HOLY TRINITY SUNDAY
JOHN 16:12-15

A MYSTERY

Of all the theologians I read regularly, I think the religious writer who most consistently delights me is Peter Marty, son of longtime Lutheran writer Martin Marty. Like his father before him, Peter appears in *The Lutheran* magazine every month. For me, his article is usually the highlight of the magazine.

One month, Pastor Marty spoke of prayer as a conversation with God, not as much a chance to get to know God as it is a chance to enjoy God. In prayer we celebrate our relationship with God while deepening it. On this Trinity Sunday, I would like to ask you something about your prayer life.

If you want to address God in your prayer conversation, are you more likely to address God as "Father" or as "Jesus" or as "Spirit"? In the sample prayer that Jesus gave us, he started with "Our Father…." It would certainly be appropriate to address God this way in prayer.

At the same time, my favorite hymn is "Beautiful Savior," which is really a prayer to Jesus, Son of God and Son of Man. Praying to Jesus is a long-standing tradition in the Christian faith. In his letter to the Philippians, Saint Paul writes that God gave Jesus "the name that is above every name, so that at the name of Jesus every knee should bend… and every tongue should confess… that Jesus Christ is Lord" (2:9-11). The power of using Jesus' name in prayer is best exemplified in the Roman Catholic and Eastern Orthodox tradition of the "Jesus Prayer." In order to open up their hearts to God and

17

follow Saint Paul's command to pray unceasingly, penitents pray the following line over and over: "Lord Jesus Christ, Son of God, have mercy on me, a sinner."

During my first year back in my hometown of Findlay, Ohio, I was asked to perform a wedding in which the bride's family was Lutheran and the groom's was of the Jewish faith. "Could you put together a service, Pastor Bob, which would satisfy both families?" the bride pleaded. There are some things that seminary never prepares you for!

All I did was take a standard Lutheran service and change all mention of "Jesus, Son, and Redeemer" to "Lord, Father, and Creator." And — poof! — there you have it... a Jewish/Lutheran service. I thought everything went perfectly until a tiny, beautiful Jewish grandmother came up to me as I ate dinner at the reception and said, "You did a wonderful job today, Pastor. But if you ever do this again, you may not want to conclude the table blessing at the reception with, "In Jesus' name, we pray." I'd done such a good job removing our Lord from the service until I got to the one line I'd ad-libbed all day, and he sneaked back in! I can be forgiven for this lapse, however, because almost every prayer we say during Sunday worship ends with some version of "through Jesus Christ our Lord. Amen."

So there are precedents for addressing our prayers to the Father or the Son. What about dedicating them to the Spirit? Just before departing from this world, in one of my favorite Bible passages, Jesus himself told his disciples that he would send an Advocate, the Holy Spirit, who would help us in our prayers, who would intercede for us "with sighs too deep for words." The Spirit does this because we "do not know how to pray as we ought."

We have Saint Paul telling us to pray in the name of Jesus, and Jesus suggesting we pray to the Father through the Holy Spirit. What should we do? I think we should take Pastor Marty's advice and seize the opportunity we have been given to enjoy God, to delight in the Lord, to dance in the Spirit. You don't have to fully understand something to love it.

The late Cardinal Cushing once related that when he was a parish priest, he was summoned to a store to give last rites to a man who had collapsed. Following custom, he knelt by the man and said, "Do you believe in God the Father, God the Son, and God the Holy Spirit?" The man roused a bit, opened his eyes and said, "Here I am dying — and you ask me a riddle?"

It's been said that Trinity Sunday is the only Sunday in the church year that commemorates a theological proposition. The word "Trinity" appears nowhere in the Bible. The first recorded use of the Greek word "*Τριάς*" (set of three) in Christian theology came from Theophilus of Antioch in about 170 AD. To this Greek scholar, the Trinity consisted of God, God's word (*logos*) and God's wisdom (Sophia). You see remnants of this viewpoint in the beginning of John, when Jesus is called the "Word of God" (*In the beginning was the Word...*) and in today's first reading when Wisdom says that she was present before the creation of the world.

Is Wisdom the Holy Spirit? Is the Holy Spirit female? Are women wiser than men? After years of watching men leaping from roofs in homemade parachutes on the TV show *America's Funniest Home Videos*, one might be tempted to think so!

In any case, even though the Son, the Holy Spirit descending in the form of a dove, and the Father's voice were all present at Jesus' baptism in the Jordan, it wasn't until the writings of the Apostle's Creed and the Nicene Creed 300 years later that the concept of the Trinity really got fleshed out.

The Trinity is a human invention designed to help us understand what cannot be fully understood: the true nature of God. Yes, there is God the Creator, God the Son, and God the Holy Spirit, but there is only one God. Winston Churchill once famously said that Russia is a riddle, wrapped in a mystery, inside an enigma. Maybe we should revise the Trinitarian formula and baptize in the name of the riddle, the mystery, and the enigma.

Let's agree, then, that the Trinity is a mystery. We are called to engage the mystery, but we will never fully unravel it. A created being could never fully understand its creator. We don't fully understand our own minds, our own being; how could we ever fully grasp the mind and being of God? On the other hand, the concept of the Trinity gives us our best chance to begin to understand.

How do I know that this is the best approach to understanding God? Because it is the one recommended by Jesus when he said, "Go therefore and make disciples... baptizing them in name of the Father and of the Son and of the Holy Spirit" (Matthew 28:19). So, let's break down the three parts of the Trinity, and see that they are, in fact, one.

Let's start with the Father. When we pray, "Our Father, who art in heaven, hallowed be thy name," we aren't just praying to one third of the Trinity. We are praying to God the Father, God the Son, and God the Holy Spirit in very personal terms. The word Jesus uses in this prayer is *abba*, which means "papa" or "daddy," as compared to the Latin *pater*, which is the more formal "father." We are to pray to the triune (three-person) God, then, in very familiar terms. Since there are many images of God in the Bible which are feminine, we are not to think of the triune God in solely masculine or feminine terms. We are children praying to the one who creates, redeems, and protects us.

Part of the confusion surrounding God the Father results from the commonly held notion that the God of the Old Testament (who is generally connected with God the Father) is a cruel, unforgiving tyrant who is finally overcome by the loving Son, Jesus. The God of the Old Testament creates the world as something good and loves it accordingly: especially beloved are men and women, for they are made in the very image of their creator.

The Old Testament God is constantly redeeming the children of Israel, forgiving them and bringing them back into relationship. Finally, the God of Abraham and Moses is a faithful God who keeps promises and is always present when needed.

So, it isn't only the Son who'll save you, and it isn't just the Holy Spirit who will protect and guide you. Father, Son, and Holy Spirit are united in their love for you and concern for your well-being. When Jesus prays to the Father, this is very different from us praying, "Our Father" because while we are clearly children of our creator, the Son is not made but is eternally begotten (he has no beginning or end). He is, as the Nicene Creed says, of one being with the one who made all things.

The human Jesus may have been born to suffer all the ills that flesh is heir to, but the resurrected Son of God was present at creation and will be present beyond the end times. In trying to understand the Son, we are caught in a delicate balancing act: Jesus is truly human and truly divine. Make him anything less than truly human, and you run the risk of rendering the sacrifice of the cross meaningless. If the figure on the cross isn't human, there's no pain, no suffering, no doubt, no fear, and no loss of life.

If you, on the other hand, make Jesus anything less than truly divine, you run the risk of rendering the gospel meaningless. Jesus claimed to be the Son of God. Because of this, you cannot hold that he was merely a good and wise teacher. Either he was who he claimed to be, or he was a liar or a lunatic. Further, if Jesus is not the true Son of God, he cannot come again, and the good news of the gospel is null and void.

There are no half measures with Jesus: you must believe his claims completely or not at all. As I said, there is

21

no separation between the Son and Father: Jesus says that when you have seen him, you have seen the Father.

Finally, we come to the Holy Spirit. The danger inherent in the Holy Spirit is that we often try to see the Spirit as something separate from the Father and the Son. The Spirit is simply God's way of working in the world since Jesus' ascension to the Father. The Spirit is an advocate who will defend us, teach us, renew us, and unite us.

The third person of the Trinity works through our minds as well as through our emotions. The Spirit is certainly present in ecstatic prayers, faith healing, and speaking in tongues but is also evident in thoughtful Bible study, in all forms of devout worship, and in the practice of loving-kindness and charity. Again, none of this sets the Spirit apart from the Father and the Son. The Spirit is merely God's way of being in the world in the present age. Any appeal to the Spirit is also an appeal to God: God works through the Spirit.

We believe in one God: Father, Son, and Holy Spirit, as inseparable as the flame of three candles held together. Can you distinguish which part of the flame created by three candles belongs to each? In the same way, the Son and the Spirit are inseparable from the Father. *God from God, Light from Light, true God from true God*: there's no way to distinguish between them.

So why bother to speak of the Trinity at all? We speak of it because it has a past, a present, and a future. God the Father created the earth and cared for it like a mother hen watching over her chicks. God the Son took on earthly flesh with all its inherent weaknesses and endured unimaginable suffering and even death to redeem the earth and all the creatures on it. God the Holy Spirit was sent to help us hang on in the years between Jesus' death and the second coming of the Son. God is one, but we miss the vast richness of being and depth of love present in this one God if we lose sight of God's threefold nature: the glorious Trinity.

My church's mission statement calls us to move ourselves and others "one step closer to God." As we move closer to God, we feel the warm love of the one who created us, the cleansing flames of the one who redeems us, and the fiery heat of the one who wants to get us moving. If we wrap ourselves in God's love, heal ourselves in God's grace, and catch the sparks of God's passion, we will set the world on fire.

Proper 4 / Pentecost 2 / Ordinary Time 9
Luke 7:1-10

After Jesus had finished all his sayings in the hearing of the people, he entered Capernaum. A centurion there had a slave whom he valued highly, and who was ill and close to death. When he heard about Jesus, he sent some Jewish elders to him, asking him to come and heal his slave. When they came to Jesus, they appealed to him earnestly, saying, "He is worthy of having you do this for him, for he loves our people, and it is he who built our synagogue for us." And Jesus went with them, but when he was not far from the house, the centurion sent friends to say to him, "Lord, do not trouble yourself, for I am not worthy to have you come under my roof; therefore I did not presume to come to you. But only speak the word, and let my servant be healed. For I also am a man set under authority, with soldiers under me; and I say to one, 'Go,' and he goes, and to another, 'Come,' and he comes, and to my slave, 'Do this,' and the slave does it." When Jesus heard this he was amazed at him, and turning to the crowd that followed him, he said, "I tell you, not even in Israel have I found such faith." When those who had been sent returned to the house, they found the slave in good health.

BEYOND COMPREHENSION

I have several questions for you concerning the passage I just read. First, how many people do we see being healed in today's gospel? The answer: none... the healing takes place out of our vision. We don't see Jesus laying hands on the slave, or using his saliva or something else as a healing balm, as he did when he healed the man born blind, or saying something like "*Talitha qum*," as he did when he raised a little girl from the dead. These are all very memorable, dramatic moments. This story seems rather flat by comparison. Why isn't the actual healing dramatized here? Shouldn't this be the climax of the story?

I spent four years in seminary preparing for the ministry, but I spent ten years doing post-graduate work in English literature preparing for a career as an English professor. What I can tell you from all that is that when you tell a story, you want to build to your climax and then wrap the details up quickly.

The writer of Luke, on the other hand, builds to Jesus' proclamation that he's never seen such faith as that exhibited by the centurion and then just reports the healing as an afterthought: "Oh, by the way, when the messengers got back, they did find the slave in good health." Obviously, for the writer, and for Jesus, the climax was not the healing but the exhibition of faith. So, exactly how did the centurion's actions demonstrate his faith? The story is a bit awkward, isn't it?

27

The centurion had great concern for one of his slaves who was dying. He sent local Jewish leaders to Jesus to ask for help. But when Jesus got near, he sent friends to tell him not to come to his house. His explanation was that he is not worthy of Jesus' presence, so Jesus should just say the word and the slave would be healed because the centurion himself was under another's authority, and when he issued commands, people did what he said. Got it? Uh, no. I don't get it. It's passages like this one that demonstrate how important Bible study is to our understanding of God's word.

In Latin, a "century" is a tribe or company; centurions would lead anywhere from 80-1,000 Roman soldiers. Though they were subordinate to the emperor and to the generals above them, they wielded a lot of power themselves. As the centurion told us, when he said "Jump," those under him replied, "How high?" If one who was controlled by others had this kind of power, how much more power did Jesus, who wasn't subordinate to anyone, have at his disposal?

Given the social status of a centurion and that of a Jewish peasant who wandered the countryside preaching to the dregs of society, the centurion had every right to have Jesus dragged before him so he could demand a demonstration of his supposed ability to heal. Instead, the centurion meekly asked local Jewish leaders to plead his case for him. They earnestly vouched for him; after all, he had financed the building of their local temple.

Then the centurion stopped Jesus from having to enter the house of a sinful soldier and confessed his faith that Jesus was so powerful that just a word from him could bring someone who was near death back to full health. Jesus responded, "I tell you, not even in Israel have I found such faith."

My associate pastor, Paul DeMoss, once remarked that his most frequent sermon topics over his 25 years of ministry were "faith" and "peace." I think that the message I return to most frequently is a line I got from Anne Lemott: "The opposite of faith is not doubt; it's certainty." In religious discussions I have with those who don't consider themselves Christians, the most frequent sentiment I hear expressed is that if God would just appear before them, they would have faith. The truth is that if that would happen, just the opposite would occur.

If God suddenly appeared in front of us, if God performed a miracle that really could not be explained by human reason, we would be robbed of the freedom to choose to believe. There would no longer be faith because faith involves trusting what is really hard to trust. At the end of time when every knee will bow and every tongue confess that Jesus Christ is Lord because he's standing right in front of us, there will be no need for faith. We currently see in the mirror dimly, but then we will see the truth face-to-face. Faith is for the times when we see dimly.

Every morning, we rise having to trust three propositions that stretch our reason to the breaking point: Christ *has* died (the one sent by the Creator to save us allowed himself to be killed), Christ *is* risen (a man who died was raised from the dead), and Christ *will* come again (the one who died and rose will return to claim us). We are free to choose to believe or not to believe these because God has chosen to stay near but not force our acceptance.

As Jesus said to Thomas the Doubter, "You believe because you have seen; blessed are those who have not seen and yet believe." Those of us who have not seen the risen Lord with our eyes are blessed because we have opportunity to experience true faith, which is *trust* in the Lord. True faith, because it is trust and not certainty, routinely engages doubt.

Have you ever had the experience of seeing mountains from a distance? Maybe you've been out west and seen the Rockies, or maybe you've seen the Smokies down south. Maybe some of you have been to Europe and seen the Alps. When you first see the lofty peaks from a distance, it is just awesome. And I mean that literally: you are filled with awe and wonder, and experiencing what the Spanish conquistadores must have felt when they saw the Pacific Ocean for the first time. Here's how the poet John Keats recorded that historic moment: the explorers "look'd at each other with a wild surmise — silent, upon a peak in Darien." ("On First Looking Into Chapman's Homer"). The Darien mountain range is in modern-day Panama, and the shocked and stunned silence that one experiences when suddenly confronted with something in God's creation that is beyond all expression is universal.

As you see mountains for the first time or for the first time in a long time, you can't wait until you can get nearer and see them up close. But when you actually move through the foothills and reach the mountains themselves, it's always disappointing: you can't see the peaks or the clouds that cover them. The only way to actually see a mountain up close is if you are standing on another mountain as tall as, or taller than, the one you are seeking.

The most awe-inspiring scenery I have ever seen was from the area around my cousin's condo, which sits a mile higher than Denver, Colorado. Every way I looked there were mountains, stretched out as far as the eye could see. But I had to get that high to really see them.

The point I want to make with this image is that we can't truly see God as long as we are grounded in this life because God is both too large and too close. God is too large to see: there is nothing in all of creation that does not contain a piece of God, and yet God is not fully contained in any one thing: not the church, not the Bible, not our creeds, not our money or possessions, not our family, not our jobs, not our country, not our world, and not our universe. All of the things that we worship, all of the things to which we pledge our hearts, bodies, and minds, are too small to sustain us. Only God is majestic enough to carry us through life.

God is too close to see: despite being the maker and sustainer of all that is, God refuses to stay at a distance, where we might be able to get a sense of size if nothing else. The Greeks located their gods on Mount Olympus, where they could keep them contained and in view. But our God won't stay put, which is what Christmas and Easter are really all about!

Everything that was God surrendered privilege and power and compressed itself into the form of a tiny baby in Bethlehem. That baby lived a life of servitude and suffering only to be slain for the sins of others. This was all done to bring the kingdom, God's reign, here on earth and to bring the infinite magnitude of God so close to us that not one hair of our heads is unknown to the Lord of all that exists. It is impossible for us to fully grasp something that large and that close at hand.

We stand in God's foothills, and when we look up to measure and encapsulate God, we see only the rocks right in front of our face. A god on top of a mountain can be photographed; a god on a dollar bill can be measured. A mountainous God as close as our breath is beyond comprehension. Our God is like a majestic mountain that cannot be fully apprehended by those who live in its shadow.

Our God is so large and so near that we can't fully understand God's ways or mind. And what we don't understand, we naturally fear and distrust. It is in the battle between our doubts and our trust that faith is formed.

As Pastor Paul said in a sermon, to a Christian, peace isn't the absence of stress; the peace of the Lord gives us the strength to overcome adversity. When we settle into the numbing delusion of certainty, our faith stops growing.

The centurion in today's gospel had no reason to believe in Jesus or his power to save. Whatever God or gods he had been told to serve would never locate power in the meek and lowly. But the centurion trusted the God he had only recently

31

come to know and had grown a faith stronger than any Jesus had before experienced. Adversity will grow faith in us too if we can find the strength to trust that which we will never fully understand.

What would we do if Christ did appear physically in front of us and told us to serve him? Would we change our lives; would we stop spending all our time and all our energies on pursuits that will not last beyond our deaths and give our lives fully over to God? Yes, we would, but we would do so because we would then be God's slaves. What choice would we have but to serve the almighty being right in front of us?

Would there be anything inspirational, anything admirable in groveling before a master who has his foot on the back of our necks? We should thank God every day for the freedom to choose between belief and unbelief. That freedom opens the door to faith, the enemy of slavish obedience. Atheists call us mindless sheep, but thanks to a God who refuses to enslave us, who asks only for our love and trust, we are warriors who freely choose to follow the one who loves us most and has the power to protect us.

One final question on today's gospel: how did the centurion come to this epic faith? "When he *heard* about Jesus, he sent some Jewish elders to him, asking him to come and heal his slave." The centurion *heard* about Jesus: someone told him the good news, someone evangelized him, someone spread the gospel. Jesus' last command to his disciples and to us was "Go therefore and make disciples..." We Lutherans call Communion and Baptism sacraments because they were commands, battle orders directly from Jesus. But Jesus didn't say, "Go, therefore, and baptize." He said, "Go, therefore, and make disciples." Disciple-making is a sacrament, a holy calling most of us are not following. How many modern centurions are waiting for us to take this command seriously?

A final thought: when we think about God appearing before us in all glory and majesty and about how we would live our lives after that, maybe we should ask ourselves, "If we really believe that God does exist, then why are we not living that way now?"

Proper 5 / Pentecost 3 / Ordinary Time 10
Luke 7:11-17

Soon afterward he went to a town called Nain, and his disciples and a large crowd went with him. As he approached the gate of the town, a man who had died was being carried out. He was his mother's only son, and she was a widow; and with her was a large crowd from the town. When the Lord saw her, he had compassion for her and said to her, "Do not weep." Then he came forward and touched the bier, and the bearers stood still. And he said, "Young man, I say to you, rise!" The dead man sat up and began to speak, and Jesus gave him to his mother. Fear seized all of them; and they glorified God, saying, "A great prophet has risen among us!" and "God has looked favorably on his people!" This word about him spread throughout Judea and all the surrounding country.

KEEP PRAYING

*The Lord GOD has given me the tongue of a
teacher, that I may know how to sustain the
weary with a word.*
(Isaiah 50:4)

I feel that the Lord God has given me the tongue of a teacher. I've taught English to college students for over twenty years. But when I recently spoke to a weary father whose daughter had to go through a second round of cancer surgery, I found that I had no words that would sustain him. I know that as a pastor I'm supposed to have always at hand a bagful of clever and comforting phrases for those who might profit from them, but there are times when clever and comforting phrases are not only ineffective but actually dismissive and hurtful. It is better at these times to say nothing and just listen.

This father had a question for me. This question was bred from months of anguished and heartfelt prayers that were seemingly answered... and we all praised God for it... but then the cancer returned. The father's question: "What good is prayer?"

This question echoed through my head as I went to another father's visitation a few weeks later. I don't believe that I've ever known anyone who was as fiercely loyal to his family, his church, his sports teams, or his God as Gary.

37

I don't believe we can count the number of sincere, heartfelt prayers that went up when Gary needed surgery to remove a tumor that invaded his brain. But neither prayers nor loyalty prevented a second tumor from sending out its cancerous fingers that spread throughout his brain and ended his life. What good is prayer?

For that matter what good did prayer do when my associate pastor's son died after years of unimaginable physical struggle or when my wife's kidney condition became permanent? Whole congregations prayed fervently for both of them.

Today's gospel lesson is a wonderful testimony to God's power to heal, but what good did prayer do for all those who have died prematurely or for all those who continue to suffer from chronic medical conditions? What good is prayer?

There are no easy answers to this question, no clever and comforting platitudes that can be applied to the wounded like a salve. I can only tell you what prayer did for my wife and me. Sixteen years ago, Pam went into kidney failure (she was down to 12% functioning in both kidneys). When I told a friend from seminary of this, the news got out through the internet to more than a dozen other former classmates who spread the word to other pastors. The result was that probably four to five thousand people from twenty to thirty congregations all over the country were praying for her full recovery. But her kidneys didn't fully recover: the scarring was too deep. How could God not listen to all of these wonderful, faithful people?

I would assert that God was most certainly listening to Pam and me, and to all the people praying for her, and that all of these prayers *were* answered. After her prayers for healing seemed to be doing little for her peace of mind, Pam started praying for God to take the fear away and to help her deal with her condition. Almost immediately, we both turned the corner and, though the situation remained serious, it no

longer had any grip over us. We were freed by the workings of the Holy Spirit, which brought us peace, comfort,
and wholeness (*shalom*). We truly experienced healing and
not in some superficial, temporary way that would only last
until our next medical emergency. We are different people
now because we accepted the miracle God offered rather
than holding out for the one we thought we needed. Pastor
Paul had a similar tale to tell about the journey he and his
wife took with their son.

In these cases, prayer didn't bring about a cure, but it
brought healing: prayer got us all through, and it is the only
thing that keeps us going. It staves off the bitterness and al-
lows us not only to survive but to live. It's been said that
prayer doesn't change God; it changes us, and there is some
truth to that. Paul and I and our wives were transformed by
the prayers we lifted up; we are not the same people we were
before we prayed them.

Mother Teresa once said, "Prayer is not asking. Prayer is
putting oneself in the hands of God, at his disposition, and
listening to his voice in the depth of our hearts." If we think
that prayer is asking, we will frequently be disappointed. If
we put ourselves in God's hands and listen for God's voice,
we will find comfort and healing and wholeness.

It is extremely difficult for us to release control and put
our lives in God's hands. Our most impassioned prayers
come when we feel helpless because most of us have been
raised to think that we are in control of our lives. Some of
the most important lessons our parents taught us concerned
consequences.

• If you touch the stove, you will get burned.
• If you don't do your homework, you can't watch TV.
Later, these were expanded to life lessons:
• If you work hard, you will get ahead (we used to call
this the American Dream).

- Whether you think you can, or you think you can't: you're right. — Henry Ford
- The best way to predict the future is to create it. — Peter F. Drucker
- What the mind of man can conceive and believe, it can achieve. — Napoleon Hill
- If you can dream it, you can do it. — Walt Disney

All of these expressions assume that we can shape our own destinies, and it is true that we can do much to influence our futures. But God remains God still, and much of the world that God created remains mysterious and beyond human manipulation. When we are confronted with natural forces that we cannot control, we become fearful and frustrated, and we struggle to regain power. Since we can no longer keep up the illusion that we are gods, we try to manipulate the one who is God.

A friend of mine in the ministry went to visit a congregation member who was in the hospital because she had lung cancer and had a tracheotomy cut into her throat to help her breathe. When my friend walked into the room, she was shocked to see the woman smoking through the hole in her throat! As the woman sucked in another cloud of the poison that was killing her, she looked at my friend and cried, "Why has God done this to me, pastor?"

This woman who had so obviously brought all of her current woes upon herself still wished to implicate and thus manipulate God. Sometimes I find myself lifting an imaginary cigarette to my throat as a symbol of the human desire we all feel for self-justification, denial, and desire to control God.

The apostle Peter correctly answered Jesus' question, "Who do you say that I am?" (Mark 8:29). "You are the Messiah," Peter declared. Peter was delighted that he had been blessed to follow the one who was to lead the people of Israel out of bondage into freedom. The Jewish people had been waiting for the Messiah, the powerful king who would establish God's reign on earth, and Peter was proudly serving that king.

But Jesus told Peter to keep what he knew a secret and then proceeded to tell him what being the Messiah really meant. "The Son of Man must undergo great suffering, and be rejected by the elders... and be killed, and after three days rise again" (Mark 8:31). Suffering, rejection, death: Peter didn't think he'd signed on for this! He expected an end to suffering; he expected glory and power. He rebuked Jesus, and Jesus told him his words were devilish.

Peter thought to gain some control in a dangerous world by his association with Jesus. When Jesus made it clear that the future would be even more out of control, he rebuked Jesus in an attempt to manipulate him. We do this all the time in our prayers, don't we? We bargain, we complain, we accuse, and we beg.

Let me make this clear: there's nothing wrong with asking God for help. There are many places in the Bible where God's heart and/or mind are moved. In today's gospel, Jesus was moved by compassion to heal the only son of a widow. Is there any more tender line in the entire Bible than this one: "Jesus gave him to his mother"? Abraham bargained with God for the city of Sodom: "What if ten righteous people could be found there?" And God agreed, but there weren't ten, and the city was destroyed.

God certainly is always moved by prayer, and we all know of instances when God answered prayers. But the choice of response always rests with God: God is not our servant. The only drawback to democracy that I can think of is that we don't have much experience with being servants. Here's lesson one: servants don't tell the king how to be king.

God must be an awfully patient monarch to put up with our arrogance. The narrator of the psalms bargains, complains, and accuses God of unfaithfulness: "You have prospered my enemies while making me a laughingstock.

41

Everyone keeps asking, 'Where is the God of Israel?'" And God always waits patiently until the psalmist finally runs out of gas and says, "But I will trust in the Lord because his promises are good."

Whenever my young niece would ask for something her parents didn't want to or couldn't give her, my brother-in-law would say, "Someday." If she asked for a pony or an expensive doll or science kit (she is now a very successful engineer), Dean would nod his head and say, "Someday." And somehow, this always worked. She seemed satisfied and would go on with whatever she was doing. I kept telling Dean, "You know there will come a day when she comes to you and says, '*Now* is someday, Dad. Where's all my stuff?'" When we don't get what we ask for in prayer, God says, "Someday." And the day is near... "when he will wipe every tear from [our] eyes. Death will be no more; mourning and crying and pain will be no more" (Revelation 21:4).

In the meantime, trust what's hard to believe sometimes... and keep praying! God will surely lay his hand on the funeral bier on which we have capitulated and say to us and to those who would mourn for us, "Do not weep." And then he will tell us to arise and live again.

Proper 6 / Pentecost 4 / Ordinary Time 11
Luke 7:36—8:3

One of the Pharisees asked Jesus to eat with him, and he went into the Pharisee's house and took his place at the table. And a woman in the city, who was a sinner, having learned that he was eating in the Pharisee's house, brought an alabaster jar of ointment. She stood behind him at his feet, weeping, and began to bathe his feet with her tears and to dry them with her hair. Then she continued kissing his feet and anointing them with the ointment. Now when the Pharisee who had invited him saw it, he said to himself, "If this man were a prophet, he would have known who and what kind of woman this is who is touching him — that she is a sinner." Jesus spoke up and said to him, "Simon, I have something to say to you." "Teacher," he replied, "speak." "A certain creditor had two debtors; one owed five hundred denarii, and the other fifty. When they could not pay, he canceled the debts for both of them. Now which of them will love him more?" Simon answered, "I suppose the one for whom he canceled the greater debt." And Jesus said to him, "You have judged rightly." Then turning toward the woman, he said to Simon, "Do you see this woman? I entered your house; you gave me no water for my feet, but she has bathed my feet with her tears and dried them with her hair. You gave me no kiss, but from the time I came in she has not stopped kissing my feet. You did not anoint my head with oil, but she has anointed my feet with ointment. Therefore, I tell you, her sins, which were many, have been forgiven; hence she has shown great love. But the one to whom little is forgiven, loves little." Then he said to her, "Your sins are forgiven." But those who were at the table with him began to say among themselves, "Who is this who even forgives sins?" And he said to the woman, "Your faith has saved you; go in peace." ... Soon afterwards he went on through cities and villages, proclaiming and bringing the good news of the kingdom of God. The twelve were with him, as well as some women who had been cured of evil spirits and infirmities: Mary, called Magdalene, from whom seven demons had gone out, and Joanna, the wife of Herod's steward Chuza, and Susanna, and many others, who provided for them out of their resources.

PROPER 6
PENTECOST 4
ORDINARY TIME 11
LUKE 7:36—8:3

TRUE MIRACLES

Every time I've cut my hair since March, more of my beautiful brown curly locks have been relegated to my stylist's floor and more of these gray roots have shown forth. Being a pastor is making me old! I used to put a rinse on my hair so I wouldn't look like my wife's father. I've turned sixty this year, and it is time to put away the things of childhood, like Justin Timberlake's hair! If you don't know who Justin Timberlake is, you're older than I am!

One aspect of being old is that you start to look back into your childhood. When I do this, I often think about those things of today that would have surprised me the most as a young man. What miracles would sixty-year-old Pastor Bob have to share with fifteen-year-old aspiring writer for *Rolling Stone* magazine, Bobby Cochran, other than the fact that he was to become a pastor?

The first miracle is my phone: where are the cords, the dial, the ear and mouthpiece or the cradle? When I was young, I loved to look up at the sky and try to locate stars and constellations. I'd pull out astronomy books (and, no, they didn't light up at night) and stare blankly at a seemingly random mess of twinkling dots. Some ancients used to believe that there was a blanket between heaven and earth, and the stars were pinprick holes in that blanket through which the bright light of heaven shone. Poetic, isn't it? The stars might as well have been random holes for all I could make out.

Now, I pull out my telephone (that statement itself would have made no sense to fifteen-year-old Bobby) and open up my *Star Walk* app, which identifies every star and constellation. I can not only tell you what constellations are above us right now, but I can describe what people on the other side of the earth are seeing as well!

Speaking of miracle apps, I spent all of my childhood listening to the radio trying to figure out the name and performers of one song or another. I would have never believed that I could hold my phone next to my car speakers and have it not only tell me the name of the song and the artist, and put the lyrics on a screen that scroll down with the song as it plays, but with a single touch, I could connect to the internet and download that song onto my phone so I can play it through my car speakers at any time. The Jetsons never had technology this good! (You don't remember the Jetson's cartoon? Maybe I am getting old!)

There are other miracles of the modern age as well, of course. Who would have believed that we would be paying for water in the new millennium? A comedian once speculated that two Frenchmen were sitting at dinner in Evian, France, and one turned to the other and said, "You know how stupid I think Americans are? I think we could get them to pay for their water!"

"Miracles" have become commonplace today. Do we still need real miracles? In one of his sermons, my associate pastor asked a really important question: "Can there be hope without miracles?" My short answer to Pastor Paul is, "Yes, there can be… absolutely."

Don't get me wrong, we all pin our hopes on miracles from time to time, and I've seen God enter into situations when hope is all but gone and deliver life-altering miracles in answer to heart-wrenching prayers. We've seen this happen in my church, and it's always such a powerful experience.

46

We return to those times often when God feels distant and confidence wavers.

I want to tell you about a man from my parents' congregation in Whitehouse, Ohio. Dick and his wife were always extremely active in the church, always willing to offer their home for meetings, bring food for a dinner, organize a fund drive, and drive kids to a youth gathering. When I lived at home before entering seminary, Dick was in his late forties and played a mean second base on our softball team. One Sunday, Dick stood up at announcements (which came at the end of the service) and told us all out of the blue that he had been diagnosed with incurable cancer, and he was given less than a month to live. We were stunned; nobody knew what to say.

He told us that his favorite song had always been "Jesus Loves Me" and asked if we would sing it at the end of each service as long as he was alive. So every Sunday at the end of announcements, with his wife and little boy and girl sitting in the front row, we sang "Jesus Loves Me," as Dick grew weaker and weaker in the hospital. Most Sundays, it was nearly impossible for us to finish it. If it hadn't been for the booming voices of the children of the congregation, we probably wouldn't have. But we kept singing it every Sunday.

The next summer, when I looked over at second base, Dick was there. Not in spirit — I mean, Dick was really there! The cancer suddenly went into remission just at the time he was to die, and he had practically no long-term effects from it. So, how's Dick today? Well, he read the lessons for my ordination service, and I see him every time I visit my parents. He's grown older, but he's lived a full life.

There isn't one person in that congregation who doesn't realize we were part of a miracle. Were we able to pull it off because of our great belief in God and the power of prayer? No, if we would have had those, we wouldn't have had such

47

a hard time getting through that song every Sunday. We were sure that Dick was going to die and didn't believe that the song would make any real difference to his health, but it did have a profound effect because we trusted enough to give it all over to God and sing that song, no matter how silly it might seem to do so.

And God decided to show us something: God decided to demonstrate that every miracle in the Bible is possible. Jesus didn't calm the storm; walk on water; raise the dead; feed thousands; and heal the sick, the lame, and the possessed so that 2,000 years later we could see these as clever metaphors. The storm got calmed; the seas got walked on; the dead got raised; the thousands got fed; and the sick, the lame, and the possessed got healed through the power of God, through the living Christ.

But what are we to make of those times when a miracle is not forthcoming, when people fall to their knees and pray, but the worst case scenario happens anyway? Spouses are widowed; parents are left childless; seniors lose their mental faculties; diseases and afflictions become chronic; careers, homes, and pensions are lost. Is there anyone here who thinks that these tragedies don't happen to good Christians? Sincere prayers rise up to heaven each time, but miracles do not always rain down on the frightened and hurting.

Jesus healed many in his ministry, but he didn't heal every cripple, every blind man, everyone battling demons. Many people died in Jesus' lifetime, but he only resuscitated one son, one daughter, and his friend, Lazarus. Jesus wasn't a faith healer: he didn't promise a cure for every ailment as payment for the right contributions. Jesus' miracles were signs of who he was and proof of his compassion. He didn't come to eliminate death and disease and suffering but rather to show us that these have no power over his followers.

If our hope can't rest on God's performing miraculous cures and interventions for us, in what can we trust? Let's look at another miracle or two, including the one in today's gospel.

Pastor Paul tells the story of a nurse who cared for his son at the end of his life. Paul wanted to show his gratitude, but when he tried to find her, there was no record of her: she ministered to his son and provided comfort and protection in a time of need, and then disappeared without a trace.

This story shouldn't surprise us because the Bible tells us that we should always be kind to strangers for we never know when we will find ourselves unknowingly entertaining angels. If God's messengers are occasionally sent to test one's hospitality, it seems only natural that they would also be employed to minister to those in need.

The miracle here is not that there are angels active in the world — angels seem no less believable than the devil, and we all *know* Satan exists — the miracle here is one of presence. God was truly present with Pastor Paul's son, just as God is always present in times of great need. Presence is one of the miracles that God promises every time we pray. In his last words to his disciples, Jesus promised to be with us always, "even unto the end of the earth" or "the end of the age" in our translation. In other words, God will be with us until the end times, and then we will be with God for all time.

So if you ever find yourself arguing, bargaining, or pleading with God at some time of great stress, recognize that the real miracle is that God is there. The one who is so far beyond our comprehension is so near that we can feel the warm breath of the Spirit against our skin. Pray for God's presence, and you will never be disappointed.

A second miracle God delivers every time we pray for it can be seen clearly in our gospel. A woman, who is not supposed to even touch men like Jesus, makes an extravagant show of submission in front of everyone at a dinner. She falls to the floor behind him as he reclines on cushions at the table, removes the sandals from his dusty, road-weary feet, wipes her tears from them with her hair, and then anoints them with expensive oil. Propriety and pride have been thrown to the winds because of the gratitude she feels at having been absolved of her sins.

Circumstances had no doubt forced her into the shameful life of prostitution, and either Jesus or his mentor John the Baptist had absolved her, had freed her from having to continue this life or carry the guilt it entailed. A self-righteous Pharisee at the table scoffs to himself that the Son of God would know that this woman was beneath his contempt and make her stop her gaudy display. But Jesus knows his thoughts and answers his unspoken condemnation: those who have been forgiven extravagantly display gratitude extravagantly. "Those who display as little respect and appreciation as you have shown me," Jesus is saying to the Pharisee, "have obviously not been the recipients of much forgiveness."

In speaking of this lesson, C.S. Lewis once said that "Prostitutes are in no danger of finding their present life so satisfactory that they cannot turn to God: the proud, the avaricious [greedy], the self-righteous, are in that danger."

The miracle here is not that Jesus knew the Pharisee's thoughts but that he forgave a repentant sinner. He offers us that miracle every time we pray, every time we confess our sins, every time we forgive those who have wronged us. "Can there be hope without miracles?" My short answer is yes, but my longer answer is no. Because true faith means trusting, especially when God does not move heaven and earth for us, we can rejoice that God gives us the chance to choose to have or not have faith. But without the miracles of God's presence and forgiveness, we would be truly lost.

Proper 7 / Pentecost 5 / Ordinary Time 12
Luke 8:26-39

Then they arrived at the country of the Gerasenes, which is opposite Galilee. As [Jesus] stepped out on land, a man of the city who had demons met him. For a long time he had worn no clothes, and he did not live in a house but in the tombs. When he saw Jesus, he fell down before him and shouted at the top of his voice, "What have you to do with me, Jesus, Son of the Most High God? I beg you, do not torment me" — for Jesus had commanded the unclean spirit to come out of the man. (For many times it had seized him; he was kept under guard and bound with chains and shackles, but he would break the bonds and be driven by the demon into the wilds.) Jesus then asked him, "What is your name?" He said, "Legion"; for many demons had entered him. They begged him not to order them to go back into the abyss. Now there on the hillside a large herd of swine was feeding; and the demons begged Jesus to let them enter these. So he gave them permission. Then the demons came out of the man and entered the swine, and the herd rushed down the steep bank into the lake and was drowned. When the swineherds saw what had happened, they ran off and told it in the city and in the country. Then people came out to see what had happened, and when they came to Jesus, they found the man from whom the demons had gone sitting at the feet of Jesus, clothed and in his right mind. And they were afraid. Those who had seen it told them how the one who had been possessed by demons had been healed. Then all the people of the surrounding country of the Gerasenes asked Jesus to leave them; for they were seized with great fear. So he got into the boat and returned. The man from whom the demons had gone begged that he might be with him; but Jesus sent him away, saying, "Return to your home, and declare how

51

much God has done for you." So he went away, proclaiming throughout the city how much Jesus had done for him.

PROPER 7
PENTECOST 5
ORDINARY TIME 12
LUKE 8:26-39

PLAYING IT SAFE

I am here today to tell you that a great fraud is being perpetrated in my hometown. Ever since I returned to Findlay, people have been telling me: "Join the Y, and you'll get in shape." So I finally joined the Y (I'm old enough to remember when it was called the YMCA!) a year ago, and I have to tell you, it has done me no good. It would serve them right if I'd actually enter the building for the first time and tell everyone there that they are being duped! Joining the church and refusing to go out and spread the gospel is like joining the Y and staying home. All the health benefits go to those who get off the couch and get in the game.

I was thinking about cardinals the other day, not the kind who wear red robes but the kind that sit in trees. Now, if you've ever wondered what it's like to have the mind of an artist or writer, those of us who have such minds are right now imagining high officials in the Roman Catholic church wearing their high hats and all of their bright silk finery sitting in trees! It's pretty entertaining having such a mind, but one is terribly distracted most of the time!

Anyway, I was thinking about cardinals the other day. While the evolutionary process God created decreed that nearly all of the other birds would don feathers that matched their surroundings to keep them safer from predators, the cardinal went the other way. Now, I know what you're thinking, "Hey, what about blue jays? They're colorful." Yes, indeed, they are, but their evolutionary safeguard is that they are just plain nasty!

When my family lived on South Main Street here in Findlay, Ohio, across an alley from Jefferson Elementary School, a family of blue jays decided to move in to one of our neighbor's trees. Our neighbors developed the habit of running from their garage to their back door with their hands over their heads because Mama Jay didn't like people in her babies' nursery!

God-ordained evolution also gave jays the nastiest scream on God's good earth. Cardinals, on the other hand, have voices that sound like the angels singing in perpetual spring.

"Well, what about orioles and scarlet tanagers?" you ask. Okay, this is a sermon, not a lecture for the Audubon Society. We're talking about cardinals and jays here.

One of my greatest delights returning to my hometown and taking a call at First Lutheran is that the congregation really seems to enjoy learning and being challenged to think. I taught at four different universities for over twenty years, and I preach at a higher level here than what I taught there. But there is a challenge here as well: I can't get away with anything! There's always someone here who will think of orioles and scarlet tanagers. And it would be one of these brilliant teenagers the congregation is raising that would point it out to me. Actually, it'd probably be a precocious eight-year-old: I always have to watch out for them!

I was thinking about cardinals the other day — how *do* cardinals survive? Hawks can see the color red, and unless one is color-blind, male cardinals stand out like a sore thumb. Now there are various possible scientific explanations out there:

• Birds see differently than we do; maybe what's bright to us isn't bright to them.

• The color red is absorbed by the color green, so maybe a green woods hides the cardinal. Did you ever see a scarlet tanager in a woods? I didn't think so.

• Hawks can see a whole range of color, but their favorite prey tends to have muted colors. They can see a cardinal, but red is not necessarily a food color to them. Even though I can see it on my plate, I don't eat purple food!

Two friends of mine in Athens, Ohio, used to sing on stage a beautiful Mexican-style ballad they wrote. I always liked to hang around after their performances to watch the dreamy-eyed freshmen girls come up to them and ask what the English translation of the song would be. They were always crushed to hear that the song was titled, "Why Are There No Blue Vegetables?" If I had a plate of blue vegetables, I doubt if I would eat any of it. Maybe hawks just don't like red food.

All of these explanations are fine as far as they go, but the truth of the matter is that natural selection operates on a cost vs. benefit system. Whatever cost the cardinal pays for its bright raiment, it is more than made up by the advantages its color gives it in mate selection. Females have no problem finding males in the cardinal world.

Women complain all the time: "I just can't find a good man." Maybe single men should dress in bright red: it certainly works for cardinals! If there are a hundred birds in a field, a female cardinal can pick out the five male red birds before you have time to say, "Get me to the church on time." Is that reference too dated?

So I was thinking about cardinals the other day. In the cardinal world, it is more important to be attractive than safe. When it comes to evangelism — spreading the good news of Jesus Christ — we Lutherans, like those of many mainline denominations, have been playing it safe for a long, long time. We wait for people to come to us… here, in church, and then we count on the pastor to proclaim the gospel.

55

It's dangerous to mention God, Jesus, the Spirit, or the church out in the world. Even in here, if we come off too strong, people will think we're weird. I wouldn't want anyone to feel like we might be different, but I have to say that the God we worship gave us one command before leaving this world: "Go, therefore, and make disciples" (Matthew 28:19). How do you make disciples? Jesus' last words in the book of Mark are these: "Go into all the world and proclaim the good news to the whole creation."

What good news? "For God so loved the world that he gave his only Son, so that everyone who believes in him may not perish but may have eternal life. Indeed, God did not send the Son into the world to condemn the world but in order that the world might be saved through him" (John 3:16-17).

The problem is that our faith is tepid — neither hot nor cold. How will a tepid faith save us when trouble comes? My associate pastor asked a very interesting question during his Pentecost sermon: "The Holy Spirit has fallen upon you through the word, through the sacraments, and through music: what are you going to do, just go on with business as usual?"

How do shy Christians evangelize? I think that the best strategy is summed up in one of my favorite hymns: "I Love To Tell The Story." Everyone you know and meet has a God-sized hole inside that only God can fill. Help them by telling them how God is filling that void inside you. You never know when your story could bring someone one step closer to God.

A recent poll showed that only 2% of Lutherans have ever shared their faith. The Holy Spirit has gifted and restored each of us, and we each have a story to tell. We just need to figure out our faith story and tell it to others. The Holy Spirit will do the rest! As Jesus told the man whose demons he had exorcized, "Return to your home, and declare how much God has done for you" (v. 39).

In closing, I'd like to quickly mention four lessons we can take from today's story of the healing of the Gerasene. First, though the man, while under the influence of the demons, resisted him in the beginning, he ended up sitting contentedly at Jesus' feet: fully healed. It is better to be tormented by God than soothed by the devil we know.

Second, our God has power over all demons. Our personal demons are in some ways as real as this man's, but they certainly aren't as powerful. He was possessed by a legion of demons potent enough and maddening enough to send a whole herd of pigs over the edge of a cliff, yet they were no match for the Son of God.

Third, Jesus healed by his presence. There are no magic incantations here, no calls for penance or even repentance before healing can take place. The man was first healed by the very presence of Jesus in his life; then he turned his life around.

Finally, we are not called to merely accept Jesus into our lives and live with him; we are called to go out and tell the world what God has done for us. Jesus turned down the man's request that he be allowed to stay with his master and then redirected him to the place where he could do the most good. The man who could not live in the company of human beings was now going home to declare his love for the one who saved him to all who will listen. We too can be freed from our cages by the presence of Jesus in our lives.

Those of us who have been freed need to get going. It is no good making a shrine of our opened cages. We need to take the key (the love of Christ) from the door and go release those who are still trapped.

Proper 8 / Pentecost 6 / Ordinary Time 13
Luke 9:51-62

When the days drew near for him to be taken up, he set his face to go to Jerusalem. And he sent messengers ahead of him. On their way they entered a village of the Samaritans to make ready for him; but they did not receive him, because his face was set toward Jerusalem. When his disciples James and John saw it, they said, "Lord, do you want us to command fire to come down from heaven and consume them?" But he turned and rebuked them. Then they went on to another village. As they were going along the road, someone said to him, "I will follow you wherever you go." And Jesus said to him, "Foxes have holes, and birds of the air have nests; but the Son of Man has nowhere to lay his head." To another he said, "Follow me." But he said, "Lord, first let me go and bury my father." But Jesus said to him, "Let the dead bury their own dead; but as for you, go and proclaim the kingdom of God." Another said, "I will follow you, Lord; but let me first say farewell to those at my home." Jesus said to him, "No one who puts a hand to the plow and looks back is fit for the kingdom of God."

FREE FROM WHAT?
FOR WHAT?

Today's readings give us a chance to talk about freedom quietly a week before advertisers and politicians can fill the airwaves with patriotic rhetoric designed to sell us everything from washers to "wisdom" from Washington. We call the Fourth of July "Independence Day" and have good reason to celebrate. We say this is the day we gained our freedom from British rule. But are the words "freedom" and "independence" really synonyms?

I would maintain that, though we did gain our independence from England in 1776, we remained largely English for some time after. If we had truly become something new in the eighteenth century — Americans — we wouldn't have viewed native Americans as the enemy. But we continued to think of ourselves as Europeans and held on to our hatred and fear of everything non-European for a long time. Most of us still identify ourselves more readily with European culture than with the culture of the people who occupied these lands before us. We weren't free of the English in the 1770s; we merely became independent of them.

In today's gospel, Jesus was approached on the road by three unnamed people of unspecified gender. Often it is the case that when an unnamed character appears in the gospels, that character is meant to represent us. We are the ones who approach Jesus and tell him that we want to follow him but cannot walk away from the lives we are leading. We say we want to be given time to put our affairs in order, to take care of those we love, to say good-bye to friends and family. But the truth is that we really don't want to let go of what we have, and we do not want to commit ourselves fully to God. Jesus' demands for total commitment seem stifling and unfair. Such a radical commitment to serve someone else goes against our nature as freedom-loving Americans.

In the second reading for today, Saint Paul tells us, "For freedom Christ has set you free. Stand firm, therefore, and do not submit again to a yoke of slavery" (Galatians 5:1). This sounds like something the framers of the Declaration of Independence would say, doesn't it? But Paul goes on, "For you were called to freedom, brothers and sisters; only do not use your freedom as an opportunity for self-indulgence, but through love become slaves to one another" (v. 13).

Oops, it seems we've been made free only so that we can enslave ourselves. This sounds ridiculous to our ears because we think of freedom and slavery as opposites. The truth is that independence and slavery are opposites but, as I said, freedom and independence are not the same thing. One can be independent and yet not free, as was the case of the early Americans who were not free from European assumptions and prejudices; and one can be free and yet enslave oneself to others, which is what Paul and Jesus are calling us to do.

We live in a society that worships independence. We have long prided ourselves as being a nation of rugged individualists. We love to hear stories of people who have bucked the system and overcome great odds to get what they want. We constantly preach on the importance of gaining independence from parents, siblings, and peers. We say a person must be physically, intellectually, and emotionally independent in order to be fully developed. In other words, we feel we all must learn to act, think, and feel for ourselves. We must be *self*-actualized. What's wrong with this?

Teenagers have always been much maligned in this country. This is unfortunate because teenagers, like canaries in a mine shaft, can reveal much about the health of a culture. Before the age of gas meters, miners used to take canaries down into the tunnels with them because if there were any poisonous gases present, the birds, because of their delicate natures, would die before the gases became deadly to the miners. The miners could then get out before they were put in any real danger. In the same way, teens are more susceptible to the poisons present in any society. They haven't hardened themselves yet, haven't built up immunity to the toxins. If we look at how our teens are doing, then, we can pretty well judge the health of our society and what's in store for us. The problem is that for a long time teenagers have been dropping over right and left, and no one's been paying any attention.

What is it that teens have to teach us? As adults, our attempts at independence are generally balanced by our need for security: we can't walk away from our domineering boss because we need to feel financially secure. Teenagers, however, are less concerned with safety and more interested in autonomy, so they provide for us good models of what happens when our inflated notions of the importance of independence are allowed to run their full course.

In the 1960s, particularly in places like the Haight-Ashbury district of San Francisco, the streets were full of teens who had listened to all of their parents' complaints about their bosses and their constrained lives, and chose instead to live their lives differently. They decided to become completely independent; *they wanted to be free*. Instead, they ended up under the control of the people who provided them with food and shelter. They become slaves to their bodies that screamed out to be fed and comforted. They were independent, but they were anything but free.

This lesson has been repeated over and over again in the last fifty years, as teens leave home and move out to live on the streets of New York, Los Angeles, or Seattle. They are merely taking the lessons we teach of the importance of independence to their natural end. And they end up in bondage... every time.

What is true freedom? First, let me say what it is not. Freedom is not an escape from authority, from responsibility, or from obligation. Sure, authority figures, responsibilities, and obligations can feel inhibiting, but to walk away from these is to be enslaved by our bodies, our minds, and our passions. In Paul's words, it is to be enslaved by the flesh, which leads to destructive sexuality, drunkenness, the worshiping of false gods, hatred, strife, jealousy, anger, quarrels, dissensions, factions, envy, and so on. All of these arise out of our indulging our bodies, minds, and emotions.

Destructive sexuality and behaviors like alcoholism come out of our indulging our bodies rather than guarding and protecting them as one would any object of value. When we indulge our minds, they create false gods so they can feel in control of the universe. When we indulge our emotions, they invariably lead us into conflict with others. There is no true freedom until one is set free from the tyranny of one's own body, mind, and emotions. Authority, responsibility, and obligation are the keys that turn this lock.

We would all like to live lives full of what Paul calls the fruit of the Spirit: love, joy, peace, patience, kindness, generosity, faithfulness, gentleness, and self-control. But to do this, we must first be freed of the shackles of our bodies, minds, and emotions. This is not accomplished through independence but rather through dependence, total dependence on God. Love, joy, peace, patience, kindness, generosity, faithfulness, gentleness, and self-control are gifts from God.

Through Christ's sacrifice we have been set free, but from what? From the tyrannies of the flesh: body, mind, and emotions. We've been set free, but for what? We've been set free to become slaves to one another. Jesus said that he came to *serve* not to be served and that those who would lead must become servants of all. In 1 Corinthians Paul says, "For though I am free with respect to all, I have made myself a slave to all" (9:19). The irony is that only the truly liberated person can really serve others. Liberation comes when one finally releases one's own agenda and accepts God's. In our lives, we must strike a balance between security and independence, but we need to make no compromises when it comes to freedom. We are called to freedom, but we are not to use our freedom as an opportunity for self-indulgence of the flesh but rather, through holy love, we are free to become servants of God and slaves to each other.

The tale is told of British and American POWs imprisoned behind German lines in World War II and separated by a high-wire fence. The Americans had managed to create a make-shift radio and were able to get news from the outside. Every day, one of the prisoners in the American camp, who happened to know ancient Gaelic, would meet a Scottish chaplain at the fence and exchange a "greeting" in Gaelic, which would include news from the outside. The Germans never caught on to what they were doing.

One day, news of the German surrender came over the radio. The war was over, but the German guards didn't realize it for three days. During the interval, everything in the camp had changed. The prisoners were still held captive, none of the routines had changed, but they looked at their hard life differently. They sang, waved at the guards, and laughed at the dogs.

When the guards found out about the surrender, they fled, leaving the gates open. Now, when were the prisoners *really* set free? That's right — when they heard that they were to be delivered from their captivity. This is the state we live in. We are seemingly held prisoner by many things: bodies that let us down, habits we can't break, debts we can't shake, jobs we can't stand or leave, pasts we can't let go of, futures we can't fathom. But we are like the British and American prisoners: our chains can't bind us if we remember that the war is over; the victory is secured.

When Christ died and rose again, the enemy was forced to surrender. It's only a matter of time until the gates will be left open and we can walk out. Of course, there's still hardship, but we know the end now, and we know that the end is at hand. Let us live our lives in the joy and freedom of those who know the enemy is already defeated and those who know that the only true freedom lies in servitude toward God and all of God's beloved children.

Proper 9 / Pentecost 7 / Ordinary Time 14
Luke 10:1-11, 16-20

After this the Lord appointed seventy others and sent them on ahead of him in pairs to every town and place where he himself intended to go. He said to them, "The harvest is plentiful, but the laborers are few; therefore ask the Lord of the harvest to send out laborers into his harvest. Go on your way. See, I am sending you out like lambs into the midst of wolves. Carry no purse, no bag, no sandals; and greet no one on the road. Whatever house you enter, first say, 'Peace to this house!' And if anyone is there who shares in peace, your peace will rest on that person; but if not, it will return to you. Remain in the same house, eating and drinking whatever they provide, for the laborer deserves to be paid. Do not move about from house to house. Whenever you enter a town and its people welcome you, eat what is set before you; cure the sick who are there, and say to them, 'The kingdom of God has come near to you.' But whenever you enter a town and they do not welcome you, go out into its streets and say, 'Even the dust of your town that clings to our feet, we wipe off in protest against you. Yet know this: the kingdom of God has come near.' ... Whoever listens to you listens to me, and whoever rejects you rejects me, and whoever rejects me rejects the one who sent me." The seventy returned with joy, saying, "Lord, in your name even the demons submit to us!" He said to them, "I watched Satan fall from heaven like a flash of lightning. See, I have given you authority to tread on snakes and scorpions, and over all the power of the enemy; and nothing will hurt you. Nevertheless, do not rejoice at this, that the spirits submit to you, but rejoice that your names are written in heaven."

MIMOSA PUDICA

Have you ever seen a mimosa plant? When touched, the fern-like leaves of the *mimosa pudica* fold inward and droop downward. This action has a domino effect: the touched leaf folds and droops, and then the next, and the next. It looks like the plant is literally shriveling up and dying right in front of you. *Mimosa* is a Greek word meaning to mimic. *Pudica* is Latin for "shy," "bashful," or "shrinking." So, I guess you could say that the *mimosa pudica* is mimicking shyness.

The *mimosa pudica* is known by many names. In the U.S. and England it is also known as "Sensitive Plant," "Humble Plant," "Shame Plant," "Prayer Plant," "Tickle-Me-Plant," and "Touch-Me-Not." In Spanish, it is called, *mori-vivi* ("I died, I lived"). In Tonga, it is called *mateloi* ("false death"). In Hindi, it is known as *chhui-mui* ("that which dies upon touch"). In Burmese, it is called *hti ka yoan*, which means "crumbles when touched." In Indonesia, it is *putri malu* ("shy princess"). In Bengali, it is known as *lojjaboti* ("the bashful girl").

Two weeks ago, I spoke to you about evangelism. I told you that this is the way a Lutheran witnesses to the gospel: "I Love To Tell The Story." In the last two weeks, have any of you made a conscious effort to do this? Did you tell a friend or a lonely, hurting, or lost stranger about Jesus or about how the good news of God's grace has made you less afraid, or about how the church Jesus left for us has changed your life? No, I didn't think so.

There was a young preacher who delivered his very first sermon to his new congregation, and everybody thought it was a marvelous treatment of tithing and evangelism. The next week, he gave the exact same sermon, and people thought that that was a little strange, but it was a good sermon, so they let it go. When he gave the exact same sermon for the third straight week, people were furious. A committee was put together (with churches there are always committees!) and they knocked on his parsonage door. "Why have you given us the same sermon three times?" they asked. "You haven't done what I told you to do yet!" was his reply.

A recent study showed that only 2% of Lutherans have ever shared their faith, so I suppose it would be a miracle if one sermon made much difference. When it comes to sharing our faith story, why are we Lutherans (and those of many other denominations, I suppose) such *mimosa pudicas*? Are we "Sensitive Plants," "Humble Plants," or "Shame Plants"; in other words, are we too sensitive, are we too humble, or are we just ashamed of the gospel?

Are we "Touch-Me-Nots," "Shy Princesses," or "Bashful Girls"? Are we cold, haughty, or insecure? For whatever reason, we are definitely *chhui-mui*, that which dies upon touch. When the opportunity comes for us to make a spiritual connection with someone, we fold inward and shrink down. The most important thing to us in these moments is not the gospel of Jesus Christ or our mission to spread it but rather, we care only about protecting ourselves. What if our intentions are misinterpreted or we're asked a question we can't answer, or people think we're weird or obsessive, or someone yells at us or just turns his/her back and walks away?

No one knows for sure why the mimosa shrivels up at first contact. Is it worried that it will be consumed or damaged?

70

Is it shaking off harmful bugs? It also closes up if any of its leaves feels direct heat. Because it grows like a weed and has a tendency to become fuel for grass fires, it fears heat. It also fears cold: it closes up at night and opens in the morning.

We too fear that we might be eaten up, beaten up, or pestered by those we evangelize. And when it comes to the Spirit of God, we fear being caught up in the fire as much as we fear freezing to death by its absence in our lives. Let's face it, we're much more comfortable speaking of our heavenly Father than we are of speaking of the crucified Son or the Holy Ghost. But we are Christians, and you can't spell Christian without Christ, and you can't know God without knowing the Spirit that Christ sent to be with us until he returns! We must find a way to put aside our fear and move from *that which dies upon touch* to *mori-vivi* ("I died, I lived").

It takes the mimosa about thirty minutes to return to its original open state from an encounter with heat or touch. We could probably learn to shake off a bad evangelism encounter much quicker than that! Jesus told us how in today's gospel lesson.

First, he assured us that the harvest was plentiful. We do not have to go out and gather seed, plant it carefully, water it, watch over it. God has planted seeds of faith everywhere, then nurtured and guarded them. They merely need to be harvested.

So when we start to shrivel up as we face the task of sharing our faith, we need to know that the person in front of us has been carefully prepared for that moment. He/she has already experienced God: Father, Son, and Holy Spirit. The harvester merely collects the bounty from another's work.

You're not telling the people you share your faith with anything they don't already know. What you're doing is helping them understand what they've already experienced in life by making a personal connection. They see how your experiences connect with theirs and thus see theirs in a whole new light: the very light of Christ.

The British writer Ben Johnson once said that William Shakespeare's gift was that he wrote "what was often thought but never so well expressed." Shakespeare wasn't a genius because he was a master of original thought; his genius was that he mastered the art of expressing the thoughts we all have in a new, clearer way. We don't read Shakespeare to understand him better; we read Shakespeare in order to understand ourselves better. He told his stories to help us better understand our stories and our lives.

We tell our faith stories to others so they will see and understand their stories more clearly and thus see how God is working in their lives. In this way, we help them move one step closer to God, one step closer to finding meaning and purpose in life.

If we run out of personal experiences to mine for God's presence, what story do we have to tell? How about this one, from Isaiah (66:10-13)?

> *Rejoice with Jerusalem, and be glad for her, all you who love her; rejoice with her in joy, all you who mourn over her — that you may nurse and be satisfied from her consoling breast; that you may drink deeply with delight from her glorious bosom. For thus says the LORD: I will extend prosperity to her like a river, and the wealth of the nations like an overflowing stream; and you shall nurse and be carried on her arm, and dandled [bounced] on her knees. As a mother comforts her child, so I will comfort you; you shall be comforted in Jerusalem.*

We are those who love Jerusalem because we are people of the book. Their story is our story; our fate is tied up in theirs. God tells us in our times of exodus and exile, as he told the people of Israel, "Rejoice and be glad, that I may nurse you, comfort you, and bounce you on my knee like a loving mother."

My grandfather used to bounce me on his knee as he sang, "Shook, shook, shook rice. Schultz zen zie fus. Iskenbey rita bey, iskenbey dollar bey." Or some such thing. It used to weird me out something fierce!

I used to ask every person I met who spoke German what this meant, but nobody had any idea. I finally asked grandpa at the end of his life (he lived to be 100) what he was singing. It was all low German (Plattdeutsch) mixed with the fractured English of German farmers.

"Shook, shook, shook rice" is the sound of sleigh bells.

"Schultz zen zie fus" (some guy named Schultz is making a big fuss).

"Iskenbey rita bey, iskenbey dollar bey" (he bought a horse, and it wasn't worth a dollar).

Our being bounced on God's knee is nothing like my experience of being bounced on my grandfather's knee. It is the gentle, soothing, comforting actions of a loving mother: there is no confusion or disorientation or shake-up or shake-down.

God knows that we Americans are lost and frightened and shocked by what we have been experiencing as a nation since 9/11, and God wants to comfort us and nurse us and return us to joy and peace. We come here to this place to be comforted, to be fed, to rejoice, and to be glad. So God is calling us *away* from hopelessness and despair, and in today's gospel, God is calling us *into* mission.

Jesus sent out seventy disciples to heal the sick and proclaim the nearness of the kingdom. He sent them out in twos: no one was to walk alone. We heal and proclaim in community; God works through congregated people. We are sent to gather the harvest: people are waiting for us, desperate to be brought in. The way will not be easy, and we are to rely totally on God for what we need.

73

If the message is rejected, we are to simply walk away, but it is essential that we deliver it. If we do this, we will watch Satan fall from heaven like a flash of lightning, we will tread on snakes and scorpions without being harmed, we will live in the kingdom now… free from fear, free from despair, free at last, free at last, great God almighty, free at last!

What about our fears of being eaten up, beaten up, or pestered by those we evangelize? As I promised, today's gospel has an answer for that. "Whatever house you enter, first say, 'Peace to this house!' And if anyone is there who shares in peace, your peace will rest on that person; but if not, it will return to you" (Luke 9:5-6). No one can take away the peace you find in the Lord. Offer that peace to those to whom you witness: if they accept it, wonderful; if not, it returns to you unaltered. As you proclaim that the kingdom of God is near at hand, there's no time to worry about what people think of you because of your proclaiming it. After all, spreading the good news is a life-and-death matter, for the listener and the teller!

Proper 10 / Pentecost 8 / Ordinary Time 15
Luke 10:25-37

Just then a lawyer stood up to test Jesus. "Teacher," he said, "what must I do to inherit eternal life?" He said to him, "What is written in the law? What do you read there?" He answered, "You shall love the Lord your God with all your heart, and with all your soul, and with all your strength, and with all your mind; and your neighbor as yourself." And he said to him, "You have given the right answer; do this, and you will live." But wanting to justify himself, he asked Jesus, "And who is my neighbor?" Jesus replied, "A man was going down from Jerusalem to Jericho, and fell into the hands of robbers, who stripped him, beat him, and went away, leaving him half dead. Now by chance a priest was going down that road; and when he saw him, he passed by on the other side. So likewise a Levite, when he came to the place and saw him, passed by on the other side. But a Samaritan while traveling came near him; and when he saw him, he was moved with pity. He went to him and bandaged his wounds, having poured oil and wine on them. Then he put him on his own animal, brought him to an inn, and took care of him. The next day he took out two denarii, gave them to the innkeeper, and said, 'Take care of him; and when I come back, I will repay you whatever more you spend.' Which of these three, do you think, was a neighbor to the man who fell into the hands of the robbers?" He said, "The one who showed him mercy." Jesus said to him, "Go and do likewise."

BEING NEIGHBORLY

As a campus pastor in Kalamazoo, Michigan, I served on a committee that supports the local Lutheran Social Services Ministry foster care program. One Thursday, we heard about a young girl who had run away from home at age fourteen. By the time we heard about her, she was sixteen, and LSSM was trying to get her some help by putting her into an independent care program. She'd lived on her own for two years, so it seemed too late to put her into a foster care family. She would receive money for living expenses and get life skills training from a case worker. Unfortunately, she wouldn't receive her first check until the end of the month, and she'd already moved into her apartment. She needed immediate help: pots and pans, soap, toilet paper, and food. The case worker wondered if we could help set her up.

I offered to go to the food pantry at a local Lutheran church and get some groceries to tide her over. But when I got to the church on Friday, the food pantry was closed. Fortunately, the pastor was there, and he offered to help me load up a bunch of bags that I could take back to LSSM. I said, "Well, I don't know. We're both pretty busy writing sermons on the 'Good Samaritan.' Do you think we have time to help out a stranger?" God has a way of preparing pastors for their sermons — and a very good sense of humor!

As an English professor, I teach my students to try to approach everything they read with fresh eyes, as if they've

77

never seen or heard about it before. I want them to look closely at what is on the page. In this way, they can best understand what the writer is trying to tell them. Good writing is carefully crafted and can only be appreciated if it's read as carefully.

It's difficult to look at something as well known as the story of the good Samaritan with fresh eyes, but it's the parts of the Bible that have been the most used through the centuries that have been the most abused. The message has often been distorted through all the years of preachers and Sunday school teachers twisting and turning the stories to fit their own agendas. In the case of parable of the good Samaritan, years of use have turned a shocking, profound statement of the Christian life into trite moralizing. Let's look at today's gospel carefully to see what the writer of Luke really had in mind.

The first thing you notice is that the parable doesn't stand alone. Jesus had a specific purpose in mind when he told it. A lawyer had stood up to test him. To understand this, we have to get away from our notions of what a lawyer is. In Jesus' time, to be a lawyer was to be a Bible expert. The Hebrew Bible, what we call the Old Testament, was the law, and lawyers were used to interpret how the laws of Moses could be applied to everyday life.

As an expert on biblical law, this lawyer figured he would trap an uneducated Nazarene peasant in legal debate. He asked Jesus how one can gain eternal life in the kingdom to come at the end of times. You can imagine the lawyer sitting back smugly ready to attack Jesus on some fine points of the law.

But Jesus was much too clever for him: he quizzed the lawyer, *What is written in the law?* Of course, the lawyer jumped on this chance to show off what he knew and responded by giving a formula that he had memorized: "You have to love the Lord your God with all your heart/soul/strength/mind, and love your neighbor as yourself." Jesus said, "Yep, you've got it right; now, go do it!" "Now, wait a minute," thought the lawyer. "How did he get me to answer my own question?" He can't very well attack the answer he himself gave, so he figured he would have to try something else.

This time, he pulled a politician's trick: he picked out a controversial issue, figuring that Jesus would be forced to one side or the other. Either way, he would alienate some of his followers. The lawyer asked, "And who is my neighbor?" At issue here was whether Jews were to love and serve all people or only fellow Jews. Jesus could not simply ask him what the law said on this issue because the law was ambivalent. On the one hand, there were many instances in the Bible where the people of Israel were called to hate and destroy their enemies. But there were also many places in the Old Testament (like the book of Jonah) where all people were viewed as God's children and must be treated accordingly.

Jesus answered the lawyer with the parable of the Good Samaritan. The next preconception we have to rid ourselves of before we can look at this parable with fresh eyes is its title. Passages in the Bible were not titled by their authors. These titles were added much later when the Bible came to be printed and widely distributed. Just as the parable of the prodigal son is not about the prodigal son but, rather, about his older brother who refuses to forgive him, this parable is not really about the good Samaritan.

The first person introduced, the man going from Jerusalem to Jericho, is the main character of the story. We are to look at the action of the story through his eyes. Because we're told nothing about him, we know that we're to see ourselves in him. We are to see ourselves falling into hands of robbers: stripped/beaten/left for dead. The land between Jerusalem and Jericho is primarily desert and rocky ground that drops 3,300 feet in eighteen miles. And it is here, in this desolate country, that the story takes place.

And then, miraculously, we are to be saved! Here comes a priest, a temple leader. He sees us... and passes by on the other side of the road. We are surely doomed. If even a priest won't help us in our current state, we are lost, indeed.

But, look. Someone else comes; a Levite this time: not quite as holy as a priest but still a descendant of Levi and an important, if secondary, figure in temple life. But he too passes to the other side and walks on. It's obvious that we are to die here.

Finally, a third figure approaches. But what hope have we of being saved if church leaders are afraid to help us? In a final cruel irony, the third figure isn't even an ordinary Jew: he's a Samaritan. Pilgrims who passed through Samaria on their way to Jerusalem did so at peril of their lives. Why would a Samaritan stop when pious Jews would not? But he does stop, and he cares for us and sees to our recovery. This is the shock of the story that has been lost through the centuries: an enemy has stopped to help when church-going fellow countrymen did not.

It's not that this Samaritan was special: he was not meant to represent Jesus, for instance, as is sometimes thought. We're all capable of doing what he did. The Samaritan did not befriend his enemy; there was no mention that any relationship occurred between them. The Samaritan provided for the man's needs and then went back to his life's work. He would settle up the bill the next time he came through, presumably when the man was long gone. So this Samaritan isn't Jesus, he was simply a man doing what Jesus would have done.

Christian love isn't about having gushy feelings for people: it's about treating them with loving-kindness. The lawyer was made to view the situation from the ditch, and from that vantage point he saw that what defined a neighbor was neither geographical nor ethnic. Neighbors are not necessarily those who hold the same religious views as we do;

they're not just those people we like. From the perspective of the ditch, a neighbor is anyone who pulls you out: even if that person is a despised enemy.

Jesus moved from a passive definition of neighbor (one who receives help) to an active one (anyone who gives help). The lawyer's question was changed from "Who is worthy of my love?" to "How can I be a good neighbor?" Jesus' answer to this was simple. Love your neighbor as yourself: if you were in the ditch, what would you want done? Go, and do likewise to others.

My sister, Susan has a daughter named Aubrey Jo. One day, Susan was making dinner and Aubrey was in the bathroom by the kitchen. Aubrey was just learning how to use the toilet, so the bathroom door was open. All of a sudden, Susan heard Aubrey cry out, "God? God?" Susan stopped working to listen to what Aubrey would say. Again, she cried out, "God? God?" Susan couldn't take it anymore, so she said, "Well, go ahead, Aubrey Jo." Aubrey said, "God, would you wipe me?"

Aubrey's Sunday school teacher had told her that whenever you need God's help, just call out: and Aubrey knew what she needed right then! Susan came to door and said, "Aubrey, God sent me." God has sent all of us to help, heal, and spread the good news of unconditional love and salvation made possible through the death and resurrection of Jesus Christ. With the Spirit's support, we can be there for all who cry out for God's assistance. We are called and sent to be good neighbors.

I was in the parking lot of the inner city church that had the food pantry on another occasion. I was rushing to my car because I had to get back to the Western Michigan University campus as quickly as possible for an appointment when someone coming from the food pantry yelled out, "Excuse me, could you help me?"

I am sorry to say that at that time I had become so accustomed to people asking for money in that area of town that I just hurried on. I said over my shoulder, "I'm sorry, I really don't have time." The woman replied, "You don't even know what I need!" Oops, I stopped with my hand on my car door and turned back to her. It turned out that her battery was dead, and she needed a jump start. A few minutes later, we were both on the road, and I felt pretty ashamed.

Who is the neighbor? The one who helps out: me and you, all of us. How should we treat our neighbors? Like we ourselves would wish to be treated. It's pretty simple, really… but awfully hard at the same time.

Proper 11 / Pentecost 9 / Ordinary Time 16
Luke 10:38-42

Now as Jesus and his disciples went on their way, he entered a certain village, where a woman named Martha welcomed him into her home. She had a sister named Mary, who sat at the Lord's feet and listened to what he was saying. But Martha was distracted by her many tasks; so she came to him and asked, "Lord, do you not care that my sister has left me to do all the work by myself? Tell her then to help me." But the Lord answered her, "Martha, Martha, you are worried and distracted by many things; there is need of only one thing. Mary has chosen the better part, which will not be taken away from her."

PAY ATTENTION!

Many people are troubled by today's gospel. Good Christian folk are disturbed that hard-working Martha got criticized for trying to serve Jesus and wanting Mary to do her fair share. What a blow this passage is to the "Protestant" work ethic! Those who favor gender-specific roles for men and women are disturbed because the one who didn't seem to know that her place was in the kitchen was commended while the "good housewife" was condemned. Oddly enough, some feminists are also disturbed: Martha seemed to be rebuked for her sharp tongue while Mary was praised for kneeling down at a man's feet and keeping her mouth shut.

If you find yourself disturbed by this story, then you're not alone. In fact, generally, if you're not disturbed by Jesus' actions and parables, you're not paying attention. Jesus wanted to get people to look at life differently, and the only way to get people out of their old ways of thinking and begin viewing life from the perspective of the kingdom was to shock them.

Martha was a good and faithful servant. When Jesus stopped in during his journeys, she knew what he needed: he needed to be cleaned up from the dusty road, and he needed to be fed. He also needed a clean place to rest. So like the good Samaritan in last week's gospel, Martha set to work to care for the person in need.

But this week's story isn't about showing love horizontally by caring for one's neighbor. This time, we're to be told how to express love vertically (between us and God). We show our love for God in the way Mary did: by kneeling at the feet of our Lord and listening.

Let's think for a moment about the first readers of this story. The writer of Luke lived after the first generation of Christians had died. His audience had never met Jesus. They grew up hearing the stories of people who claimed to have heard him speak, or at least of people who knew people who had heard him. Can you imagine how jealous they were, how much they would have given to have actually seen him and listened to him? We'd love to sit down with Jesus too; we have a lot of questions we'd like to ask. Can you imagine how jealous we would be of someone who had actually met him?

I met Lefty Gomez once. He pitched for the New York Yankees baseball team from 1930 to 1943 and was inducted into the Baseball Hall of Fame in 1972. Babe Ruth was still on the Yankees team in 1930. It was so strange to be able to talk to someone who actually knew Babe Ruth!

Do you know what I asked him? I asked him why, on every level of baseball, the first baseman is thrown a ball by one of the coaches just before he enters the dugout! The obvious answer is that the first baseman uses this ball to warm up the other infielders between innings, after his team finishes batting. But why can't he just grab a ball for himself, or why doesn't a batboy hand him one in the dugout?

I figured that if Lefty Gomez had been associated with baseball since the time of Babe Ruth, he must have known where this odd custom came from. He thought a minute, and then said, "I don't know. I never thought about it. We have always done it, though."

Fortunately, there was also a veteran Toledo sportscaster there, who said, "That's a great question. The best guess is that it started back in the days when infielders left their gloves on edge of the outfield grass behind their positions and a coach would throw a baseball out to the first baseman when the inning was over. He would put it in his mitt and keep it there so he had a ball to use to warm up the other infielders when he returned. The practice stuck, and people were too superstitious to stop doing it."

So the ball is always thrown out before the first baseman reaches the dugout because that's the way it was always done. Obviously, the church isn't the only place where people lose track of why they do the things they do but continue doing them anyway!

Of all the things I could have asked Lefty Gomez, this was a pretty silly question. What I would have really liked to know is what sort of a person Babe Ruth really was. Did the man match his legend or were his exploits on and off the field just creative public relations? I would guess that the second generation Christians had pretty much the same questions about Jesus. Was he really all they said he was? If they could have just sat down with him for a few minutes....

Imagine their response when they were told by the writer of Luke about Martha and Mary. Jesus did visit them. And what did Martha do? She ran around like a madwoman: cleaning the house, cooking, screaming at Mary to get to work, ordering Jesus to tell Mary to help. Martha was undoubtedly a very funny character to second-century Christians. The Lord came calling, and all she could think to do was clean and cook.

Mary's response was the reasonable one. She wanted to hear all Jesus had to tell her. What Jesus was saying to Martha was, "Sit down, Martha. Listen to what I have to say. Don't yell at your sister for wanting to hear me. After all, I've come a long way."

The story of Mary and Martha, then, is funny in some ways. But it is also deadly serious. In Luke (21:34) Jesus warned that we have to be on guard that the worries of this life don't weigh down our hearts because, in this condition, the final day can come and catch us like a trap. Martha was definitely weighed down by the troubles of this life and, often, so are we.

Martha would say that a visitor needs to be fed; we would say that bills need to be paid. Jesus would say that the urgency lies with the coming kingdom not with bellies and wallets. A stomach doesn't stay satisfied very long anyway, and all that we buy with our money will pass away. We have need of only one thing: Jesus, who said, "I am the bread of life; whoever comes to me shall not hunger, and whoever believes in me shall never thirst" (John 6:35). Mary understood this better than Martha did. What Martha lacked was a singleness of vision. Jesus told her, "Martha, Martha, you are worried and distracted by many things."

How about us? Do we keep our focus on the kingdom during the week or are we *occasionally* distracted by worldly matters? How about on Sundays? Do we give even one day solely over to God and spiritual matters? Or do we have other things planned today?

We don't fight over nonreligious matters getting ready for church; do we? Surely, we've never argued on the way to church! Okay, how about one hour? Do we keep the distractions at bay for even one hour so that we can put our full attention into worshiping God? Surely we don't worry about the heat, the uncomfortable seating, what other people are doing, whether there are mistakes in the bulletin, whether we know or like the hymns, or whether the pastor went too fast, too slow, or just too long with the sermon?

I'll tell you what I think about: I want to do a good job on Sunday morning. I want to deliver a good sermon and keep the mistakes during the service to a minimum because, after all, this is my job. And sometimes, with all this attention on doing well, I forget to worship with you. Even pastors

88

struggle to give one hour to God free from the distractions of worldly things.

Let's make this very clear: the distraction is not the mistake the pastor makes, or the baby's cry, or the discomfort. The distraction is our reaction to these. We let the mistake cloud our minds, the baby's crying stir our emotions, the straight-backed pew move our thoughts from God to our bodies. Rather than looking at these through the eyes of the kingdom, we view these happenings as the world views them. To the world, a mistake is worthy of censure, a child should be seen and not heard, and physical discomfort is simply unacceptable. In kingdom thinking, mistakes reveal our common humanity, children must be heard because none of us shall see the kingdom unless we become as children, and physical discomfort is a small price to pay for spiritual fulfillment.

Those who live in the kingdom now have a single-mindedness about life. Jesus Christ is the center of their life, and all of their actions revolve around this center point. Getting back to Martha: what she didn't know, and what we forget, is that "the Son of Man came not to be served but to serve, and to give his life as a ransom for many" (Mark 10:45). Jesus came to serve by teaching and by dying for sins. In her frantic attempts to do good work, Martha was missing out on what Jesus had to tell her.

Sometimes even the good work of the church can be distracting if it interferes with one's listening to the word. There's always so much for us to do here. But we come to church so that the word of God can *happen* to us here: one word from Jesus can change us forever. This is a time when we should stop the mad dash and take time to listen.

Of course, if good deeds don't follow the time we spend here, then we have not heard. But those who attempt to do right and be "good people" without going to church or centering their lives on the gospel of Jesus Christ are like beautiful ships without rudders, moving ahead but going nowhere. "Martha, Martha, you are worried and distracted by many things; there is need of only one thing. Mary has chosen the better part, which will not be taken away from her."

Proper 12 / Pentecost 10 / Ordinary Time 17
Luke 11:1-13

He was praying in a certain place, and after he had finished, one of his disciples said to him, "Lord, teach us to pray, as John taught his disciples." He said to them, "When you pray, say: Father, hallowed be your name. Your kingdom come. Give us each day our daily bread. And forgive us our sins, for we ourselves forgive everyone indebted to us. And do not bring us to the time of trial." And he said to them, "Suppose one of you has a friend, and you go to him at midnight and say to him, 'Friend, lend me three loaves of bread; for a friend of mine has arrived, and I have nothing to set before him.' And he answers from within, 'Do not bother me; the door has already been locked, and my children are with me in bed; I cannot get up and give you anything.' I tell you, even though he will not get up and give him anything because he is his friend, at least because of his persistence he will get up and give him whatever he needs. So I say to you, Ask, and it will be given you; search, and you will find; knock, and the door will be opened for you. For everyone who asks receives, and everyone who searches finds, and for everyone who knocks, the door will be opened. Is there anyone among you who, if your child asks for a fish, will give a snake instead of a fish? Or if the child asks for an egg, will give a scorpion? If you then, who are evil, know how to give good gifts to your children, how much more will the heavenly Father give the Holy Spirit to those who ask him!"

THE TRAJECTORY OF GOD'S GRACE

When I was in junior high, I "inherited" a winter coat from my Uncle George (who is only three years older than I am). It was a very expensive coat and looked practically new, so I knew George hadn't worn it. The reason was obvious: it was an extremely thick, long ski jacket that made the wearer look like a pregnant, black polar bear. The fur that covered the whole coat had to be four or five inches long. The really sad thing was that the satin lining had a terrific embroidered snow eagle. I would have loved wearing the coat if I could have turned it inside-out. But, alas, this was impossible. As it was, my mom made me wear this monstrosity every day at a time in my life when standing out in a crowd was painful if not dangerous.

On a Friday night in December, I was invited to stay with "Billy," the son of friends of my parents. Billy was all right, but he and I were moving in different directions in junior high. While I had never gotten into trouble in school, Billy knew the principal, the vice-principal, and the guidance counselor by their first names.

On this particular night, several of Billy's friends came over. I'd never seen them before, but I could sense that we weren't going to be playing catch or watching TV. As soon as Billy's parents moved into the back room to watch television, we hit the streets. I wasn't comfortable sneaking out, so I poked my head into the room and told them we were leaving. I was hoping they'd stop us, but instead, they just said, "Well, as long as you're along, Bob, I'm sure you boys'll stay out of trouble." Ouch.

On this night, the activity of choice was throwing snowballs at passing cars. It seemed really stupid (and dangerous) to me, but they were so bad at it that nothing was coming of all their efforts. I was just glad that this was keeping them occupied. I kept out of sight and kept a watch on the time, trying to calculate when I could convince them we'd been out long enough.

And then, just when it looked like we were going to get through the night without incident, they decided that I should join them in their crime. I guess they figured I couldn't tell on them if I participated. Not that I had any intention of telling *anyone* what had happened: my parents would hold me responsible whether or not I threw a single ball, and apparently, so would Billy's. Well, they kept the pressure up until I had no choice. But I did have a plan.

I figured that if I threw behind the car, they would know I was intentionally missing, so I resolved to throw in front of the car. It would look good, and I would be off the hook. I picked up some snow and began to form it. I held onto it a long time, under the pretense of making the perfect snowball. And it was. In fact, by the time I finished with it, it was more of an ice ball, perfectly round and smooth.

Everyone insisted I join in on the next salvo and, soon, an old, beat-up tank of a car sped by. We all threw. To this day I remember the trajectory of the flight of my snowball. Time slowed down, and I watched it sail as silently and gracefully as a perfectly cast fishing fly on a hot, hushed August afternoon. The car was going too fast; every ball fell short... except the one that had been aimed to overreach. My vision shifted from the arching snowball to the speeding hulk of a car, back to the ball, ahead to the car, until it finally settled

94

on the ball as it made a perfect arch and scored a direct hit on the passenger door!

For a moment, I was frozen in astonishment and caught up in the sheer beauty of the throw. I had led the car perfectly. Nothing I had ever done in sports could match the achievement of that toss. After all, I'd only thrown once, and I had done what my cohorts had not been able to do all night. Then the car screeched to a halt, turned around, and headed our way. I ran and barely reached a large tree to hide behind. I heard the doors open, and then, nothing. I figured I'd gotten away with it. I was wrong.

Before I had a chance to move, "Jim," the scariest bully in our school, was standing in front of me. I had no chance to register the irony or unfairness of my hitting the class bully's father's car with the only throw I'd made in a town of 40,000 people, of which almost 700 were in my class, before he'd hit me in the stomach. I doubled over instinctively. And this is where my wonderful coat comes in.

With four or five inches of fur and an embroidered silk lining, I didn't feel a thing. I'd never been in a fight before and had no idea what it would be like to be in one, but somehow I'd gotten the idea that it would be more painful than this. Of course, wearing a stupid-looking coat doesn't make one stupid. I went down in a heap. Jim glared over me, made some mumbled threat, and took off before he could get into trouble for assault. I wore that coat proudly all year.

"If you then, who are evil, know how to give good gifts to your children, how much more will the heavenly Father give the Holy Spirit to those who ask him!" (v. 13).

In the spring following the snowball incident, my parents bought me a new baseball glove. This was a big deal because I had never had a new mitt before. As with many things (including a certain large black winter coat), all previous gloves had been hand-me-downs from my Uncle George. The last thing my parents said to me as I set off to play in the field behind our house for the first time was to be sure and take good care of my new glove because it was very expensive.

After playing ball for several hours, my friends and I left our gloves on the field as we always did and went off to pursue other recreational ventures. On this day, however, I forgot to get my mitt before going home. Later, when I realized what I'd done, I ran back to the field. But it was too late: the mitt was gone.

Crushed and terrified of my parents' response, I ran up to bed saying that I was too sick to eat supper. I wasn't making that part up. All night I stayed in my room panic-stricken and nauseated. I was sorry for what I'd done but also angry with my folks. To a guilt-ridden child, parents look like awful tyrants! It was one of the worst nights of my mostly happy childhood.

When I came down the next morning, mom asked me why my mitt wasn't hanging on its hook. Where was my new glove? I said I didn't know and broke down crying. I told her the whole story and apologized over and over. She smiled and pulled the mitt from behind her back! It seems she'd seen it lying on the field after I'd returned and had retrieved it. She was waiting for me to tell her what had happened.

All I had to do was come down, admit what I'd done and apologize, and I'd have gotten back the glove and not had to spend the night in my room. Instead, I spent the evening alone and miserable. My mom taught me a valuable lesson that night about responsibility and grace — someday I may forgive her for that!

In the first sermon of this series, I told you that the Holy Spirit defends, teaches, motivates, uplifts, and unites us. I experienced the first two of these roles in the two incidences I've just related. A black, furry coat may not look like a suit of armor, but it served just as well when I needed it. And the Spirit taught me a lot about grace through that baseball glove. There have been a lot of times in my life when I have felt distanced from God because of my stubborn refusal to leave my room and stand before God and admit my mistakes. In these times, I try to remember that God is grace-filled and ready to forgive: God has my back and has the glove!

Today's gospel speaks of prayer and the need to be persistent in our asking for God's good gifts. I turned sixty last summer, and this summer, for the first time, I've broken down and hired a young man to mow my lawn. Had I held on for a few more years, I could have celebrated my fiftieth anniversary of the first time I pushed a lawnmower for my father.

In those nearly fifty years, I mowed lawns in exactly the same way. I always used a push mower, and when I cut grass, I was very much an ARM. "ARM" stands for Anal-Retentive Mower, and you who are my fellow ARMs know who you are. On the first run, I would finish off all the oddly shaped corners of the yard. Then I could do the rest of the lawn in a perfect square. Basically, I took out the imperfections and the idiosyncrasies of the yard, allowing me to mow the middle part without exerting any brain power at all! You have a lot of time to think while mowing a yard, but you don't want to have to think about anything as mundane as where you should mow next.

Whenever I have told the following story about repairing the deck on my Kalamazoo house, people have assumed it was a story about a deck. Actually, it is a story about lawn mowing. My wife and I wanted to have our deck rebuilt. So we tore up all the old boards and then had a man come and hammer down new ones. I came home on Friday and saw that he had all the boards down. There wasn't any railing yet, but who needs a railing?

I got something to eat, and then went out to mow the front lawn. I filled up one bag with grass and took it to the

97

back to dump it in the woods behind our house. I walked to the end of the deck to dump the bag and then realized that though the boards were down, not all of them were nailed! The one I was standing on flew up in the air behind me, and I plunged headfirst down a fourteen-foot drop! I remember seeing the rocks coming right for me, but somehow I carried beyond them, hit the ground, and tumbled head-over-heels down the slope: avoiding trees, sharp sticks, and a lead pipe sticking out of the ground right beside where I ended up.

Not wanting to know how badly I was hurt, I decided to lay there until my wife got back from San Antonio on Sunday. Eventually, however, I got tired of lying there. I got up and found out I was fine.

I crawled back up the hill, got a flashlight, stumbled back down and found the bag, crawled back up and finished mowing the yard with the help of the front porch light. Why did I do this? Because I was afraid that if I had to go to the hospital, I might not get a chance to finish the yard for a very long time! Pam called a neighbor to come down and check on me because she was sure I had hit my head harder than I thought, but most of my ARM brothers (and sisters) probably understand.

If we are to receive all of the good things that God has in mind for us, we need to be this persistent in our prayers. Through the workings of the Holy Spirit, God will protect us, guide us, encourage us, bolster us, and unite us. These Spirit works will provide us with all we need, but we have to ask for it to be given, seek if we want to find it, and knock if we want the door to be opened.